WHAT READERS AND AUTHORS ARE SAYING

My Brave Little Man is a captivatingly detailed account of T.A. Degner's early life, beginning with his sometimes bitter, sometimes sweet rural childhood, and ending in a Dickensian description of the years he and his siblings spent in a Duluth orphanage. The story profiles an era in a setting that has not been well documented in either fiction or memoir until now. The author spins tales of his transformation from a sweet little blond cherub to a strong-willed school-age rebel. Often funny, sometimes hair-raising, it is the inspirational story of a vigorous spirit meeting multiple challenges and emerging, though somewhat bruised, as essentially whole and strong.
—**Lynn Cross, editor** (www.wingsforyourwords.com); **storyteller** (www.wildyamcabaret.org); **poet, and copywriter**

There is a wide range of emotions and traumas displayed in *My Brave Little Man*. It is a good example of how events witnessed during a child's important, formative years can affect them. Because of our age and having been adopted together, we had each other to keep the memories of our past alive; even names and actions of the children in the orphanage. We never forgot where we came from and we even remembered some of the names of our biological family members. Thank you for sharing these memories with me, Terry.
—**Jean Haraldson - Sister**

My Brave Little Man is the inspiring true story of shattered innocence. Full of spunk and determination the author shows us an interesting and compelling look at the difficult choices he was forced to make. We share his confusion as he deals with an alcoholic and absent father. We feel his pain as he courageously faces the loss of his mother. I'm looking forward to the second installment.
—**Jim Downs, author of The Book of Positive Qualities**

I thoroughly enjoyed reading *My Brave Little Man*. You can see and feel what is being described. The author walks us through his very early years, opening for us, the feelings and emotions of a young boy who was facing devastating life changes; his urgency and sense of responsibility as his mother's "brave little man!"
—**Kitty Rund - First Cousin**

Most of us grow up with a certain sense of stability that comes from a family home and loving parents. *My Brave Little Man* is a book about what it is like to grow up essentially orphaned without stability or consistency of parental love. In his memoir, the author describes, in poignant detail, how he and his brother and sister led an almost nomadic existence shuffling between family homes for brief periods, living with relatives, and ultimately to an orphanage. He describes his early life: the destitution, the abuse and abandonment by his father, his mother's lack of parenting skills and resources, the breakdown of her support system, and the lasting impact these experiences had on his life. He concludes that we must accept people for what they are—and forgive them. At the end, he and his sister, consider themselves fortunate to have transcended the early life of poverty, depravation, and abandonment. Most of us will read this memoir and realize just how lucky we really are.
—**Avron Gordon—Minneapolis**

To Barb + Dan, with best wishes.

My Brave Little Man

a memoir

T.A. DEGNER

A BANDI BOOK

Printed in the United States of America

Library of Congress Control Number: 2011905854
ISBN: 9780983663607

Terry A. Degner 1945 -

My Brave Little Man
Orders @ Bandi Publishing, www.bandipublishing.com

The Bandi Media Group LLC
15210 Lesley Lane, Eden Prairie, MN 55346

CONTENTS

INTRODUCTION

Fortunately, I don't have a memory of every minute of every day of my life. My brain is cluttered enough as it is. However, for some reason, certain events and details going back to infancy are deeply embedded. For instance, I was five the last time I saw the inside of my grandparents' house. Twenty-one years later, I described details such as the layout of the rooms, the furniture, and the wallpaper to adults who grew up in the house. They were amazed at the accuracy of my memory and confirmed much of what I told them. Though I had forgotten about the cream separator by the stove in the kitchen, they had forgotten the small mirror on the wall in the dining room.

All the events in this memoir are true. It took many years and lots of digging to find the missing pieces of the puzzle that was my life up to the age of seven. As with any neglected and aged puzzle, some of the pieces had simply vanished, some had jagged edges, and others had faded beyond recognition. All told, however, most of the pieces came together nicely. I researched old newspapers; medical, police, county, state, adoption, birth, and death records; and old telephone directories. I gathered and arranged old photographs, interviewed people, retraced my steps through terrain once travelled, and I visited institutions, homes, and even a garden where I once spent an afternoon with my mother.

At first it was impossible to put a date on many of my memories. Then, in 2007, a first cousin sent me a set of black-and-white photographs. They were duplicates of photos I received from an uncle in 1971, but many of my cousin's photos had a date and location written on the back. The dates helped me establish a time frame for events, and the name of a town on one photo turned out to be the missing piece of the puzzle that for years I had struggled with. I had remembered events associated with the town, but not its name. This allowed me to revisit the site, providing me with some details I had forgotten and reinforcing others. Some of the photos supported memories of events that took place before the age of two. For instance, I have had flashbacks of taking baths in a basin next to the kitchen sink. A photo taken when I was three shows me at Grandma and Grandpa's farm bathing in a five-gallon pail. Since Grandma and Grandpa did not have indoor plumbing, it's safe to assume that my baths in a basin or a bucket began right after birth. I have also had flashbacks of pleading with my mother to let me try on a pair of boxing gloves. I can still smell the fresh scent of tanned hide, and I can feel the smooth texture of the leather against my hands as my mother tied the laces. A photo taken when I was seventeen months shows me outside in the snow with boxing gloves pulled up to my armpits. Are the photo and the memory the same?

All of the adults connected to the early events of my life are now deceased, so I felt free to write about what happened with candor. I wrote for the enjoyment of finding the hidden truths, both within and without, but most of all, I did this for my children and for my biological mother, who deserved a better fate. I hope you enjoy reading about the journey that was my childhood as much as I enjoyed writing about it.

For my daughter's Nicole Amber, Tara Amber, and Amber Renay, You're the gifts that keep on giving. I loved watching you grow up and I'm proud of who you've become.

When asked what he had done during the Reign of Terror in the French Revolution, the clergyman and statesman Emmanuel-Joseph Sieyès (1748-1836) said, "I survived."

The author's parents Eileen Larson and Nels Haataja in 1944

Acknowledgments

A special thanks to my wife Sally, who patiently watched as I spent almost every weekday morning and many weekends at local coffee shops with a laptop as my only companion. To my sister Jean Haraldson, who traveled this road at my side. She stood up for me when others railed against me and she has been a constant source of encouragement. Thanks sis! To Alan Larson, who proved beyond a doubt that family matters. Rest in peace Alan and I'll see you on the other side.

There were other individuals who made significant contributions to the book and to them I owe a most heartfelt thanks. To Vivian Hurd, the oldest daughter of the Honkalas, who went on to become a nurse and productive member of society, despite the many adversities she faced as a child. Thanks Vivian for sharing your difficult childhood with me and for filling in the blank spaces of my father's life. She is currently working on her own memoir. Stick with it Vivian! To my dear friend and spiritual brother Jim Downs who has just completed his fourth book. Thanks Jim. I miss our Monday evening critiquing. To the women of the Ink Splotz Writing Group who put up with me for two years and especially to Jean Childers, who was the first to critique the manuscript. I think you'll find it much improved, Jean.

To Lynn Cross, an author, editor, and proofreader, who helped me with the final draft. Thanks Lynn, you were a big help.

I also want to thank some of the institutions who contributed. To the sisters of St. Scholastica, I say, God Bless. I have always felt a special bond with your order and it's as strong today as it was in 1953. To Patrica Maus, the curator of the northeast Minnesota Historical Center at the University of Minnesota in Duluth, thanks. Your professionalism and willingness to go the extra mile was a breath of fresh air. To the Duluth News Tribune for giving me permission to use a photo. To the Minnesota Historical Society who let me shift through their archives. To St. Mary's hospital, to the archives department of the Duluth police department, to the head of the Aftenro Nursing Home, and to the staff of the Northwood Children's Services, many thanks to all of you.

Almost all of the people involved with my early life are deceased. Most have been dead for many years. For that reason and for reasons of authenticity, I used full names whenever I felt it was meaningful to the story. In instances where a name was not critical, I used first or last names only. I used the last names of most of the staff members at the orphanage because that's how the children addressed them and I wanted to honor them for their service. It is possible that in some instances the names were applied to positions incorrectly. If that's the case, I apologize. I did change three staff names because they were young at the time and I was not able to verify their status. Two contributors asked me not to include their names and in one instance, I deleted a contribution because I had no direct knowledge of what happened and the facts could not be collaborated.

My Brave Little Man

CHAPTER 1

The Doctor's Wife

Cook, Minnesota, June 12, 1971. I took a right turn off Highway 53 onto First Street and slowed my red 1967 Camaro SS to a crawl, searching for a restaurant. It didn't take long. The main retail section of town was only three blocks long, and its one and only restaurant was in the center of the second block. I pulled into an open slot, turned off the ignition, and stretched to get the kinks out of my back and neck. It had been a long drive from the Twin Cities and I was tired.

"How did you ever remember the name of this little town?" my wife asked as she gathered up her belongings and stuffed them into her purse.

"I never forgot it," I said. "My sister and I talked about where we came from for years, and except for some of the buildings we saw on the highway, it's exactly as I remembered it."

"And you're sure that your grandma and grandpa's last name was Johnson?" she asked.

"No, but I think it was something simple like Johnson."

A waitress met us at the cash register and directed us to a table. We ordered and ate in silence as I thought about my next move. I knew I was born in Cook and that I had lived with my grandparents on a small farm outside of town. Were they still alive, and where was my mother? Had she moved back to Cook? When the waitress came with the check, I asked, "Did you grow up around here?"

"I've been here all my life."

"Do you know of any Johnsons living in the area?"

After thinking about it for a few seconds, she said, "I don't think so. There might be some folks who come up from the cities by that name, but as far as I know there aren't any Johnsons who live around here."

I was disappointed, but just as I was taking out my wallet to pay the bill, an epiphany struck. "Do you know of any doctors that practiced medicine here in the 1940s?"

"I don't know about the 1940s," she answered, "but Doc Heiam delivered me, and he's been the doctor in town for as long as I can remember."

"Do you know where I could find the doctor?"

"Well, unfortunately," she replied, "he's senile, but as far as I know he's still alive and living at the nursing home."

My heart sank, and I was just about to thank her and leave when she suddenly exclaimed, "But you could talk to his wife, Margaret! She was his nurse for years, and she's as sharp as a tack."

"Where could I find her?" I asked, my spirits rekindled. After all, if the doctor was old enough to be living in a nursing home, there was a good chance he had practiced medicine in the 1940s.

"Right over there," she answered, pointing through the café

window. "See the third house on that street over there, the gray and white one with the three-season porch?" Excited, I thanked her, paid for the meal, and left a big tip. "Big" is probably an overstatement, but for a college student it was big.

"Do you want to go with me?" I asked my wife as I pulled up in front of the gray and white house.

"No, I think you need to do this by yourself."

I walked up to the house and knocked on the door. Within seconds, a gray-haired woman poked her head out. "Yes, what can I do for you, young man?" she asked.

"Hi! My name is Terry Allen. I have a sister named Gloria Jean and a brother named Larry Michael…"

"Oh, my goodness, it's the Haataja children!" she exclaimed. "I was your nurse when you were born, and I'm your grandma's sister. Do you remember your grandma?"

"A little," I answered, "but I don't remember her name."

"Lillian. Her name was Lillian, and your grandpa's name was Nels Larson."

CHAPTER 2

The Nest

Cook, Minnesota, August 25, 1945. I arrived eight months after my parents, Niilo Haataja (nicknamed Nels) and Eileen Larson, tied the knot and, as luck would have it, just in time for a light lunch. "Master Terry Allen Haataja" is what my mother wrote on the first page of my baby book, and under the heading of Remarks she wrote, "He is always happy and smiling with very cute dimples and big blue eyes." Photos, and what little information I have been able to find about my parents' courtship, suggest that conception most likely occurred in Duluth. Why I was born in the hospital at Cook and why I lived with my maternal grandparents for the first two years of my life is unknown.

My sister Jean arrived at 10:15 on the evening of October 18, 1946. On the first page of my baby book, our mother added an entry for "Mistress Gloria Jean Haataja". She did not write anything under the Remarks heading, but in small print in a column to the left of the entries she had made for me she noted the date and time and Jean's weight and place of birth.

How my mother managed to get pregnant with my sister is a mystery. From all accounts, our father did not live with us. He lived either in Cook or with relatives in Tower, a town not far away. Family members would later tell me that my grandparents refused to let him stay at the farm, and photos seem to confirm this. I have one of him with my mother and me at the lake when I was a baby, suggesting occasional contact, but there are no photos of him at the farm.

My mother did not spend a lot of time at the farm, especially on weekdays. I say this for two reasons: First, what few memories I have of nurturing do not involve my mother, only Grandma. I sense my mother's presence, but I have always had this feeling that Grandma was the primary caregiver. Second, the photos show my sister and me playing outdoors in our underwear or in our grubby clothes, with Grandma working nearby. When our mother is included, she is dressed to the hilt and posturing for the camera, suggesting that she may have worked in town or at a resort on one of the many lakes in the area. My best guess is that her brother drove her to and from work and that she spent most of her evenings and weekends at the farm, but for reasons that will become obvious, she continued to have a relationship with our father.

My mother's parents, Nels and Lillian Larson, owned a small thirty-acre farm located between the town of Cook and Lake Vermilion, arguably the most beautiful lake in the state. They were opposites in many ways, but they seemed to be suited for each other. At least, I don't recall any major arguments or blowups over finances or any of the other domestic issues that destroy so many families today.

They had raised four children. Alan, their only boy, was the only child still living at home when we arrived on the scene. He did most of the physical labor on the farm, which didn't amount to much, as only ten of the thirty acres were cleared. Grandma and Grandpa's oldest daughter, Rhoda, and my mother's twin sister, Irene, had moved out in the early 1940s and were living and working in the Duluth area.

Grandpa towered over everyone, including Uncle Alan. He had to remove his hat and bend over whenever he entered the house to avoid hitting the top of the doorframe. Uncle Alan, who was six-two, looked to be about two inches shorter in photos, so that would put Grandpa somewhere around six-three or four. Grandpa was skinny, with narrow shoulders and a small waist. His face was thin and weathered and he had a firm jaw, large nose, and squinty eyes that made him look as if he had been staring at the sun too long. Except for those times when he entered the house, I seldom saw him without his hat, even at the kitchen table. Once I asked Grandma why he always wore his hat, and she whispered conspiratorially, "I think your grandpa is embarrassed about his shiny head."

Grandpa had a great sense of humor. He loved to tell jokes and stories. During lighter moments, he would speak with a thick Norwegian accent. When the conversation turned serious, his accent would abruptly disappear. Sometimes he would become downright cynical, especially when he talked about "city folks." I remember one conversation at the kitchen table when he lectured Jean and me about the trees. "You kids are too young to remember the way it used to be," he began. "Heck, my kids are too young, but at one time the trees around here were gigantic. They were so big it took a full day just to cut one of them down. They were all hardwoods, not the soft junk you see around here today. New growth, hah! That's what they call these saplings. They can't even protect us from the cold winds blowing in from Canada. They'll most likely cut them down before long to make more toilet paper for all those city folks who come up from Minneapolis." Fishing was another of his favorite topics. "Those city folks are the ones taking all the fish out of the lakes, you know!" he would exclaim. "At one time, I could go out on the lake for an afternoon and bring home a string of walleyes. Now I'm lucky if I catch a perch." Sometimes, if he really got rolling, he would go into the growing traffic problems and all the new cabins the city folks were building around the lakes. I would sit there with my chin resting on my hands, taking it all in.

[I inherited Grandpa's sense of humor and his accent. In my early twenties, I went through a phase where I would tell Ole and Lena jokes at social gatherings into the wee hours of the morning. On rare occasions, I still use the accent, but I seldom tell the jokes. As for the cynicism, perhaps I inherited a little of that too, as I do have a sense of doom about the misuse of the world's natural resources. But that is a subject for another time and place.]

Grandpa may have had the size, but Grandma was in charge of the house. At five-foot-four, with petite but hard features, thick, unruly, graying hair, and distended ankles, she ran the household with an iron fist. Serious and demanding, both of herself and others, she went about each day focused on her chores. She seldom smiled, but she was a good listener, and beneath her stern and sometimes gruff exterior, she had a genuinely warm heart and gentle spirit.

One of my first detailed memories is from the summer of 1947. I loved Grandma's cookies, especially chocolate chip. They melted in my mouth—that is, if the chocolate made it past my face and clothes. One day after Grandma went outside to do the laundry, I decided to make an assault on the cookie jar. I opened several kitchen drawers and, using them as a ladder, climbed to the kitchen counter, balancing myself as I skirted the sink—not an easy task for an almost-two-year-old. I reached in, grabbed a cookie, and bit into it. To my astonishment, it was not chocolate chip, but raisin, which, as far as I was concerned, was like going from cake to mashed potatoes. Jean started to beg me to throw one down to her, but before I could, Grandma walked in. "What are you doing on the counter, young man?" she shouted as the screen door slammed behind her.

Startled, I almost lost my balance. "I just wanted a cookie," I said, knowing I was in deep trouble.

"Well, you don't get cookies that way. You ask first. You could have hurt yourself getting up there like that. Do you know how dangerous it is to do what you did?" she demanded, grabbing me off the counter. She got out the butter paddle, laid me over her knee, and spanked me until my bottom turned red and I started to cry. Afterwards she said, "I'm sure that hurt, but it would have hurt a lot more if you had fallen and cracked your head wide open." She may have been right, but I didn't see it that way—not at the time anyway.

[I have inherited Grandma's work habits and her serious nature, which, when combined with Grandpa's sense of humor, is a worthy combination, but I have stayed away from corporal punishment. The mother of my three children asked me to spank our oldest daughter once. It hurt my sensibilities so much that I told her not to ever ask me to do it again, and she never did.]

For many families, the second half of the 1940s was a time

of celebration. The nation had just won two major wars, one in Europe and the other in the Pacific, and it was entering a time of renewal and growth. Money and jobs were in great supply, new homes were going up everywhere, and cars were on the verge of growing wings. Almost every home had electricity, running water, radios, and a few even had television sets. While the rest of the country moved toward prosperity, however, Grandma and Grandpa remained stuck in the Great Depression. When I watch old black-and-white reels of life in Appalachia during the Prohibition era, it reminds me of life on the farm. We were isolated. Meals were prepared over a wood-burning stove, laundry was done by hand, and light came from candles or kerosene lanterns. Going to the bathroom meant a long hike to the outhouse or, at night, a five-gallon pail. Since Grandma and Grandpa didn't have a telephone, they had to drive into town to communicate with the outside world.

Winters were especially difficult. The living conditions were harsh and, at times, unforgiving. A potbellied stove in the dining room and the wood-burning stove in the kitchen were the only sources of heat. In the middle of the night, someone, usually Grandpa, would get up to stoke the fires. On many winter mornings, I would come down to breakfast and see a thin sheet of ice in the water bucket next to the kitchen stove.

Despite the lack of modern conveniences and the harsh climate of the north woods, I don't remember ever going without food or the other necessities of life. We ate fish and lots of small game such as rabbit, duck, and goose. When Grandpa or Alan shot a bear or a deer, they skinned and dressed it right there on the farm. Occasionally Grandpa would kill one of the chickens that nested in the barn, or a pig, but most of the meat came from the surrounding woods. I remember many a conversation around the kitchen table about the taste of the meat—had it been corn-fed or had it lived off the bark of trees?

I can't say with certainty that Grandma loved to cook, but I can say with absolute authority that she was a *good* cook. Her desserts, pies especially, were delicious. I loved her strawberry-rhubarb pie, which she made with the wild berries my sister and I helped pick from the floor of the surrounding woods. The aromas of her piecrust and fresh bread overpowered all the other odors in the house. We had caramel rolls, cake, or pie with every meal, and I always ate dessert first, a practice that will most likely go with me to the grave. If a host makes the mistake of putting dessert on the table with the rest of the food, rest assured it will disappear first.

Besides baking, Grandma pickled or canned everything. Because the farmhouse didn't have a basement or a cellar, her stewed tomatoes, green beans, rhubarb sauce, and an assortment of other canned vegetables and berries were stored in anything cool. During the spring thaw, Grandma would put the jars in the ditch alongside the driveway, but usually she stockpiled them in the creek that ran through the woods about a quarter mile from the house. She would tie a string around the neck of the jars and drop them into the hole Grandpa had dug for her. Then she would tie the other end of the string to a stick she had pushed into the mud at the edge of the creek.

When my baby sister Jean and I weren't eating or sleeping, we played in the house or outdoors with whatever happened to be handy. On nice days, I would often pull her around the back yard in a rusty old Radio Special wagon, the one Grandpa found at the town dump. Old car parts and rusty farm implements were scattered everywhere in the back yard, and unless Grandma specifically outlawed it, I would find creative ways to turn the object into a toy. Rolling old car tires around the yard was especially fun, and I spent hours sitting on the seat of Uncle Alan's old rusted bike, which leaned against the side of the garage. Most of the time, however, Jean and I played in the dirt by the back door. This way, Grandma could keep track of us from the kitchen window. Several photos show Jean and me playing with a blue Morton Salt container, which looked the same then as it does today. I remember filling the container with dirt and making little piles in the path leading up to the house, which Grandpa had to walk around or step on when he came in for the noon meal.

"By golly, Grandma," Grandpa said in his heavy Norwegian accent, "I tink da gophers are making mounds in da yard den. I better get out da traps and get doze liddle buggers."

"It wasn't gophers, you silly," I said. "We made them," and everyone had a good laugh.

When it rained or snowed, we played inside. Because we didn't have many toys, we would often end up in the kitchen banging on pots and pans with a wooden spatula. I got into everything not attached to the floor, driving Grandma crazy.

She continually warned Jean and me about staying close to the house. One day Grandpa put the fear in us. We were all sitting around the kitchen table when he said, "By golly, Grandma, did you hear about da neighbor's baby den?"

"No, what about the neighbor's baby?"

"Vell, I yest heard 'bout an eagle dat came by and snatched a baby right outta da stroller when da mudder vasn't lookin'." By this time, my ears were burning and my eyes were bulging out.

"You mean it picked up the baby and carried it away?" I asked.

"You betcha," he said. "I've heard of eagles carrying off full-grown dogs."

"What do they do with them?"

"Vell, dey feed dem to dere chicks."

"Did they eat the baby?" I asked, fear beginning to take hold.

"Vell, I don't know, I yest heard bout it da udder day," he answered, "but I tink da two of you better stay close to da house for da time bein', don't you?" I nodded in agreement, and from that point on my sister and I seldom strayed far from the house without an adult nearby.

Seldom, however, is not an absolute, and I didn't have to go far to get into trouble. The back yard, littered with used boards, broken glass, rusty pails, and old car parts, was an accident waiting to happen. One day I decided to venture into the garage at the end of the driveway, and like most of the other buildings, it had not been childproofed. My sister, who had learned to walk at nine months, followed close behind. "No go!" Jean scolded, trying to sound like Grandma.

"Stay by the house," I said, pointing my finger at her.

"No...you!" she said, biting her fingernails.

The garage door was open, so I walked in, but she held back, afraid of both what Grandma would do if she caught us and of the eagle swooping down to get her. Two deep ruts in the dirt floor of the garage were evidence of its past use, but now they were both smooth, an indication that Grandpa hadn't parked the car in the garage for some time. A workbench littered with old parts in various states of disrepair ran the entire width of the garage, and I spotted an object that looked somewhat like an old rusty bike, except that it didn't have wheels. I had seen Uncle Alan use it once to sharpen the scythe he used to cut grass. On one end of its heavy frame was a steel tractor seat. On the other end, instead of handlebars, a large gray circular object, maybe three inches thick and twenty inches in diameter, stood upright like the head of a horse. Under the tractor seat were bicycle pedals. I climbed on and put my feet on the pedals. Then I reached out and touched the side of the gray object. It was cold and coarse and hard like a rock; hints of rust and silver glistened in the light from the open door. A steel platform or shelf not more than four inches square was fastened to the frame next to my hands. Pretending I was riding a bike, I put both of my hands on the shelf to steady myself. Then I stood up on the pedals and pushed.

I'm not sure how I got my wrist caught between the shelf and the sandstone grinder, because everything happened so quickly, and I don't remember the trip into town or the doctor visit, but after all these years, the stitch scars on my wrist are still clearly visible. I also recall Grandpa or Grandma saying, "I bet you won't do that again," and something about the "cut going to the bone," but I don't believe I got a spanking. They probably thought my injury was punishment enough.

As I look back at those years, I'm not sure how I survived, or maybe I should say I'm not sure how Grandma survived, because I drove her nuts with my questions, and I never sat still. Anything that came into my path was fair game to be taken apart, banged on, picked up, tasted, shaken, or squeezed. Whenever I was silent for any length of time or if I made a move toward something that wasn't permanently attached to the floor, Grandma would shout, "Terry, what are you getting into?" Once, I shoved a bean into my ear so deeply the doctor had to remove it with a tweezers. I was climbing before I could walk, which would certainly help explain all the things I got into. I was walking by eleven months and potty-trained before the age of two. I have other memories of those first two years, like taking baths at the lake, pulling leeches off my legs, and jumping off the end of the dock into deep water with the full expectation that Uncle Alan would rescue me. None of these experiences, however, prepared me for what would come next.

CHAPTER 3

The Real Family

Somewhere around my third birthday, Jean and I left Grandma and Grandpa's farm to live with our parents. I have no memory of the circumstances leading up to the move—no family discussion, no fanfare or warning.

Grandma, who had been unusually quiet at breakfast that morning, got up to wash the dishes, while our mother stayed at the table with Jean and me. "Children, I have something exciting to tell you!" Mom said with an enthusiasm normally reserved for holidays. Your dad is coming to pick us up. He's going to take us to live in a big city and we're going to live in a real house with running water and electricity! What do you think about that?"

I didn't know what to think. Was she saying Grandma and Grandpa's house wasn't real and we wouldn't be living with them anymore? "How come?" I asked.

"Because your dad got a job with a big company," she said proudly, "and we get a house to live in. You want to live in a real house like other families, don't you? You can't live with Grandma and Grandpa forever."

"I don't want to go! I want to stay here with Grandma and Grandpa!" I shouted.

All of a sudden, Grandma slammed something down on the counter and in a commanding voice said, "Terry, enough! You need to do as your mom says. Go upstairs with her right now and get your things together." Stunned by both what she said and how she said it, I obeyed. In hindsight, I understand the wisdom of her actions. Grandma knew me. She knew I would get even more upset if Mom continued to talk about leaving. Maybe this was also her way of dealing with her own pain. She had raised us from birth, and now she was losing us.

I watched as Mom did all of the packing. Afterwards, we went downstairs and sat at the kitchen table to await the arrival of our father. We didn't have to wait long, which was a good thing, because I don't think I could have withstood the antici-pation. He arrived mid-morning, circled the yard, and pulled up in front of the house. The greetings were stiff and terse. When he got around to me, he smiled and said, "Well, hi there, young man, you remember your old man, don't you?" I did, of course, and nodded without saying anything. It wasn't one of those "this is your father" moments. I didn't have any specific recollections of things we had done together, other than im-ages of him sitting in a bar and working in a welding shop, but I knew that he was my father, that he talked with a strange dialect, and that every other word coming out of his mouth was a swear word. Bad language was not something Grandma tolerated in her house, and she hated it when Dad used the term "old man" when referring to himself. "Your father is your father," she would say, "not your old man. I don't want to ever hear you say that." When he finished loading the luggage into the car, he bent down and picked me up. "Up you go, young man," he said.

That's when Grandma blew up. "You're not planning on putting that child into the rumble seat, are you?" Grandma shouted to my father as he stood next to his 1931 Ford Sports Roadster. "Those seats are not suitable for children."

"They'll be just fine," Dad said as he reached for Jean and dropped her in. "I'll drive slowly and keep the back window open. That way, Eileen can keep them under control."

"Eileen!" Grandma almost shouted, "Are you buying into this nonsense?"

"Nels, they can sit on my lap," Mom said in a submissive voice. "They're small and I'll keep them out of your way."

"Fine!" he said in a huff, putting Jean down on the ground. "We'll all sit in the front, but you better keep the kids away from the gear shift." When he lifted me out, I stumbled and fell to my knees in the dirt. Irritated, he said, "Go to the other side of the car and sit with your mother."

"Don't be rough with those children," scolded Grandma, "they didn't do anything to deserve that kind of treatment."

"What did I do?" my father asked, throwing his arms in the air.

"You threw him to the ground!"

"Mom, I'm sure he didn't mean to do that," my mother said. "Terry and Jean, come over here. You can both sit with me." I sat on the edge of the seat with my knee next to the gearshift, being careful not to hit it. Jean sat on Mom's lap. I heard Grandma say, "We'll see you at Thanksgiving." They waved as our father put the car in gear, and within seconds, we were speeding down the driveway and away from the little farm and the security of the only world I had ever known.

That incident and the drive to our new home is the first solid memory I have of my father's physical presence. I can still feel his strong arms lifting me in and out of the rumble seat, smell the musty scent of his sweat-soaked clothes, and hear his Finnish accent. On the drive we stopped at the Great Laurentian Highland Divide sign that stands alongside the highway between Cook and Virginia, Minnesota. Our mother took a picture of our father holding Jean on his lap with me standing under the sign. As we were getting ready to leave, I noticed a picture painted on my father's left arm. Pointing at it, I asked, "What's that thing on your arm?"

"A tattoo of an anchor."

"What's this?" I asked, running my finger around his sweaty forearm.

"A chain holding the anchor."

"How come you have it?"

"I was out with some of my Army buddies one night, and they dared me to get a tattoo of a Navy anchor, so I did."

"Did it hurt?"

"No, I didn't feel a thing," he said, laughing.

As we resumed our journey, my mother said, "Kids, aren't you excited? We're going to be a family and live in a real house just like real people do." It was the same comment she had made at the kitchen table that morning, but this time I felt a strange irritation creep over me. The reference to "kids" bothered me because Grandma never allowed anyone to refer to us as kids. "They're children, not goats," she would scold. The "real people" comment, however, was the biggest slap in the face. I had grown up with Grandma and Grandpa. To me, they *were* real people and they *did* live in a real house. In retrospect,

I think Mom said this to make it all real in her own mind. It's a saying she would repeat often, and for me, it would come to symbolize the hopelessness of her circumstances.

CHAPTER 4

The Real House

The "real house" was in a small community southwest of Duluth called Morgan Park. Named after U. S. Steel's founder, J.P. Morgan, the village was set on a high bluff overlooking Spirit Lake. It had started out as a planned community for the employees of Duluth Works, a mill owned by U. S. Steel. In 1933, the company deeded the village to the City of Duluth, so by the time we arrived, the community was open to anyone.

The schoolhouse in the center of town is the most dominant image I have of Morgan Park. (Oddly enough, the image itself is not even a childhood memory, but instead it comes from one of the many out-of-body experiences I had as a teenager. I see myself from a distance sitting on a tricycle, watching children playing on the school grounds during recess. Why the memory emerged in this way is a mystery. No photo exists of that particular image, as it was not in the collection I received. I have only the memory, but it is as clear as any photo could ever be.)

Today, new additions, probably dating back to the 1960s

or '70s, flank the old schoolhouse, but the playground in the back is still the same, and the outline of the original building is clearly visible.

The complex we lived in bore some resemblance to a loaf of bread, with our two-story unit being an end slice. Our "end unit" was definitely not the house Mom had envisioned, and it wasn't the largest dwelling I had ever been in, but it was the newest. Not that I had been in lots of dwellings during my short journey on this planet, but it would be many years before I would live in anything as comfortable. The rent and the furnishings were most likely part of my father's employment package. The unit was confining, however, even for someone my size. The front door opened into the living room. A staircase that started just inside the door took up a good chunk of the room, leaving just enough space for a couch, one sofa chair, and a coffee table. It looked more like an extra-wide hallway than a living room. A dining table separated it from the kitchen. There were only two windows on the first floor. One was in the living room and the other overlooked a small fenced-in patio, which opened onto an alley, a parking lot, and the backs of other units.

The upstairs consisted of two bedrooms and a bath. Jean slept with Mom and Dad in their room, and I had the second bedroom to myself. This arrangement was a first for me, as I had always slept in the same room as my mother and sister. The bedroom was narrow and windowless, but unlike the slanted ceiling in our bedroom at Grandpa and Grandma's, the ceiling in my new room was horizontal, allowing adults to move around freely. Carpet covered the floor and instead of an Army cot, I slept in a real bed with a spring and mattress. I also had my own standup dresser and a small closet, but the thing that stuck out the most was the smell of newness. I don't know if we were the first occupants, or if it was just simply a fresh coat of paint, but it's a scent I wouldn't experience again until I bought my first new car in 1967, and I wouldn't have a bedroom as new and comfortable as this one until the early 1970s.

The amenities throughout the unit were luxurious compared to those at the farm. Instead of kerosene lamps we had electric lights, and instead of taking baths in a basin next to the kitchen sink or in a barrel in the middle of the kitchen floor, we had a real bathtub and hot and cold running water. Playing in the warm, sudsy bathwater was a new experience for me, and I put up quite a fuss whenever Mom told me to get out. Sometimes she would indulge me and let me stay in the tub so long that my fingers looked all wrinkly, like raisins.

Flushing the toilet was another fun little thing for a boy of three who, up to that time, had effectively lived in an earlier century. I had been potty-trained on a five-gallon pail and an outhouse that was hot in the summer, cold in the winter, and smelly all year long. On top of that, I was accustomed to wiping my bottom with old newspaper or magazine pages, so the feel of soft toilet paper and the sound of a toilet flushing were new experiences for me.

Comforts maybe, but there were few, if any, decorations. Except for the clock on the wall between the living room and the kitchen, the rooms were sterile: sheets covered the windows and the walls, and the tables and dressers were bare. It's possible that my parents hadn't been together long enough to accumulate pictures, bric-a-brac, or frilly lace curtains, but I think there was more to it than that. If my mother had one overriding trait, it was cleanliness. She kept the house tidy to a fault, picking up after me before I could even make a mess.

It was this trait, more than time or money, that gave the unit a sterilized look and feel. It wasn't unusual for me to leave a toy on the floor for a trip to the bathroom and return to find it had been put away.

It didn't take long for my true character to emerge in our new house. According to medical records, I was taken to St. Mary's Hospital in Duluth on August 29, 1947, with "second-degree burns due to boiling coffee over the anterior thorax." I had forgotten about the incident, but when I read the medical file, I had one of those "Oh, yeah, now I remember" moments. The accident happened shortly after we moved in. Mom had poured herself a cup of coffee, set it on the kitchen table, and returned to the stove. I moved awkwardly over to her chair and brought the cup to my lips. One sip and it went flying, the scalding liquid spewing down the front of my shirt.

Despite these adventures, I can't say that Mom's "real house" ever became a home. It had the physical comforts of a modern house, but unlike the farmhouse, it didn't radiate warmth. It wasn't a nest, it was a *ledge,* and as such, we were vulnerable, but before any more drama could play itself out, I returned to the farm for more scars.

CHAPTER 5
Blind Disobedience

A few months after moving into Morgan Park, we returned to the farm for Thanksgiving. Mom, Jean, and I took the Greyhound to Cook, and Grandma and Grandpa met us at the bus stop. Dad stayed home. On the way to the farm, Grandpa told me about a litter of baby kittens living in the kitchen. Cats ran wild on the farm, and I remember thinking that it was unusual for Grandpa to keep them as pets, but the thought didn't prevent me from getting excited about the prospect of playing with them.

I can still picture the car lights of Grandpa's Model A as they penetrated the darkness with a hypnotic glow. I can smell the mustiness of the interior and hear the grind of the engine and the vibrations and rattles as the car shattered the deathlike silence of the north woods. The drive took fifteen minutes on a good day, not because of the distance, which was only five miles, but because of the many ruts in the narrow dirt road that snaked to the farm. "I can't wait to play with the baby kittens!"

I said gleefully, rubbing my hands together and bobbing up and down on the back seat. "Can I name them?"

"Of course you can," Grandma said, "but first you have to sit down. I'm afraid you'll go flying through the roof if Grandpa hits a rut."

"I can't fly through the roof," I said. "It's too hard, you silly."

"No, maybe not, but you could get a big lump on your head," countered Grandma, her voice stern.

"Or you could put a big dent in da roof den," joked Grandpa, and everyone laughed. As if on cue, the front tire hit a large rock in the road and the car recoiled, sending bodies flying. The adults grabbed for something to hang onto while I flew up in the air, almost hitting the ceiling, and I landed in a heap in the back seat.

"Careful, honey," said Mom as she reached out to support me. In her right arm, she cradled Jean.

Moving closer to my sister, I leaned over and said, "I get to name the baby kittens." Jean stared at me with a dazed look, not saying a thing. She had fallen asleep right after we left town, and except for a murmur or two, she had not stirred, not until the excitement of hitting the rock.

"Here we are," said Grandpa as he pulled into the driveway and parked in his usual spot by the fishing shack. Before he could turn the car off, I opened the door, hopped out, and bounded toward the house, my little feet barely touching the ground, my mind focused on the kittens.

"Don't run, you'll trip and get hurt," Grandma shouted after me. A full moon and the headlamps from the car lit my way as I scampered through the junk that littered the yard.

"Terry, do as your Grandma tells you!" shouted Mom. Paying no heed, I continued my mad dash to the house and rushed headlong inside. Except for a small glimmer from the windows in the kitchen, the room was pitch black, so I never saw the object lying in wait for me on the floor. Hitting it in full stride, I stumbled and flew forward, my arms flailing wildly, trying desperately to keep my balance. I landed headfirst with a thud against something sharp and hard. My head snapped back and I felt a sharp pain. Then everything went black. I awoke with a throbbing headache and my forehead hurt something awful. Grandpa was cradling me on his lap and Grandma was holding a dishtowel against my forehead. Mom stared down at me with a terrified look.

"What happened?" I stammered, finding it difficult to focus on the faces staring down at me.

"You fell and hit your forehead," said Grandma curtly. "Grandpa and your mom are going to drive you into town to see the doctor. Here, Eileen, keep that towel against Terry's forehead so it doesn't start bleeding again."

"What will he do?" I asked apprehensively.

"I don't know, but he needs to look at that cut," said Grandma. "It's pretty bad. You may need some stitches."

"Will it hurt?"

"No, the doctor will give you something so it won't hurt. Besides, you're a big boy. You can handle it."

[The doctor had delivered both Jean and me, and his nurse was Grandma's sister, Margaret. They had been Beatty girls before marriage, and the Beatty homestead was just down the road from Grandma and Grandpa's farm. The Beattys came from a large clan of Irish immigrants who migrated to Canada in the early 1800s and then to Minnesota in the early 1900s.]

When we got to town, Grandpa went straight to the doctor's house. The doctor came out to the car and lifted the towel.

"You say he fainted," the doctor said, concern on his face.

"Yes, he was out for maybe a minute," answered Mom.

"I'll meet you at the hospital, Nels," the doctor said. "He'll have to have stitches, and I want to do some tests to make sure it isn't a concussion." Turning to me, he said, "You got quite a cut there, Terry. Why did you go and do something like that?"

"I don't know," I answered, embarrassed.

At the hospital, Grandpa carried me into a small room and laid me on a table. The doctor said something about keeping me still, and Aunt Margaret wrapped me tightly in a blanket. The doctor put some kind of metal cone with a paper thing-amajig on it over my nose, and I fell asleep.

I don't remember much else, but I do recall hearing something about sixteen stitches, and I did get to name the kittens. Years later, someone told me I had hit my forehead against the legs of the cream separator by the kitchen stove. I had always thought that I had hit the stove leg. A photo taken in the fall of 1947 shows me standing in the driveway at the farm, a Band-Aid prominent on my forehead. The wound left a scar like a bolt of lightning, and when people question me about it, I tell them the story of Thanksgiving at the farm.

CHAPTER 6

A Family Portrait

Almost all of the memories I have of my father come from the time we spent together as a family in Morgan Park, although a few of them, especially those relating to his character, come from remarks I had overheard at the farm. Both sets of memories, however, are quite clear and both reinforce a one-sided negative portrait of him. The memories I have of my mother, on the other hand, are less slanted and more tranquil, but they are incomplete and vague.

Physically, Mom was the opposite of her twin sister, Irene. Irene was tall and slender like Grandpa, but Mom was petite and shapely like Grandma. Even the twins' hair and facial features were different. Mom had a high forehead, a small recessed mouth, and dark brown curly hair; Irene had light brown wispy hair and a large symmetrical face. Both women had deep blue eyes and Grandpa's bulbous nose, and both took great pride in their clothes and appearance, which came, I suspect, from growing up in poverty.

I have tried to remember my mother's presence from that time: the sound of her voice, a smile, a hug, or a kiss, the smell of her perfume or the touch of her hand, but without success. This may have been due to the times, as families were not as demonstrative as they are today, but there may have been other, more salient, reasons. Quiet and unassuming, my mother was indecisive and dependent on others for meeting many of life's routine challenges, like driving or family finances. Even as a child, I could sense there was something different about her. In my teens, when friends would ask what my real mother was like, I would say, "She wasn't the brightest bulb on the Christmas tree." I didn't fully understanding the significance of those words at the time, but they would prove to be perceptive.

Mom had an unusual quirk in her choice of clothes for me. Jean and I had grown up playing in our underwear or in hand-me-downs. I'm not sure what her motivation was or how she got our father to fork out the bucks, but for the first and only time in my life I became a walking fashion statement. Photo after photo shows me dressed to the hilt in sailor outfits. Button-down pants, white tops with blue trim and a flap in the back, and a blue peacoat gave me that "sailor on leave" look. The only thing missing was the white sailor hat. Instead, I wore a beanie that made me look like a miniature nineteenth-century frat boy.

Her cooking skills were another matter. Our meals were always the same: Cream of Wheat for breakfast, soup or peanut butter and jelly sandwiches for dinner, and hot dogs or macaroni and cheese for supper. Jean and I were used to Grandma's homemade bread, her sweet rolls, and especially her pies, not to mention the large variety of meats.

As I mentioned before, when it came to picking up after us,

Mom was a fanatic. It wasn't unusual for me to return from outside or the bathroom to find the toy I had been playing with missing. When I would ask her where it was, she would simply say, "I put it back where it belongs." It was an annoying habit, but one that I quickly adjusted to, even going so far as to hide the toy behind the couch or to bring it with me.

As a disciplinarian, Mom seldom, if ever, raised her voice; she never resorted to spankings, and I don't recall her ever asking our father to punish me. She would send us to our room for quiet time, but that was the extent of it. I say *us*, but in truth, it was always me, because Jean was perfect—just ask her. Kidding aside, as nearly as I can remember, I was a polite and well-mannered toddler with an inquisitive mind and lots of energy. I had a bad habit of getting into things, but I was not malicious or destructive.

Bulldog is the word that comes to mind when I think of my father's physical attributes. His body was solid and round; his head, shoulders, and hips all looked to be about the same in diameter. Contrary to this unflattering description, however, some women, including my mother, considered him handsome. He wore his hair short; they called it a crew cut or butch in those days, and he often wore brown-tinted sunglasses that matched his rugged, suntanned complexion.

My father didn't display affection or demonstrate love, he never read to me, and he never played with me, but his insulting manners, his pretentious bragging and cursing, and the musty smell of his clothes and rough, grease-encrusted hands, a result of driving and working around diesel engines all day, are constant memory markers of him.

When we had company, he would often lift me up in the air, toss me around, and say, "You're just like your old man, aren't you?" Then, without any further affection, he would put me down and go back to his drinking. He was also an artist at offering, and just as quickly taking away, small treats. and, when sober, he made promises he never kept.

[Despite all of his character flaws, I didn't hate him. My grandparents taught me not to hate, and I am eternally thankful for that. I did not, however, look up to him like so many of my peers did to their fathers. In fact, I have spent a lifetime reacting negatively, sometimes even physically, to any male with even a trace of his mannerisms. Once, in grade school, a young boy kept bragging about his father, the Greyhound bus driver. Maybe the stories of his father's exploits were true but, to me, his manner of speaking brought back memories of the way my father spoke. Finally, I told him to shut up. It's one thing to be proud of someone you love, I thought, but I had the feeling the boy was stretching the truth to the point of absurdity. I felt sorry for him later and I knew that I shouldn't have jumped on him. Not long after that, his family moved, and I regret not having had the opportunity to apologize or, to at least, find out what was really going on in his family.]

Why I should remember my father's and not my mother's persona in such detail is perplexing, considering the short amount of time we all lived together. Even then, I was never alone with him. I think his place in my memory is due to his "bigger than life" personality. The motorcycle daredevil Evel Knievel comes to mind when I think of a flamboyant personality, but Knievel was a successful man of action, whereas my father's personality was what I call "vain audaciousness." As long as his alcohol level was elevated to that of a normal drunk, he was charming and full of himself, even generous, but if it rose any higher, he turned into a monster—like Jekyll and Hyde.

Once, during one of his less than sober moments, someone asked him for the time. He said, "It's f***ing time for you to get a f***ing watch!" and then he laughed, oblivious to the man's feelings. Even at my young age, I knew that was wrong.

As for abuse, I have no proof or memory of physical abuse in our household, although I think my father did come close to being a perpetrator. He swore and yelled, and at times he threw things in the house, but other than the threat of violence, I don't recall seeing him strike my mother, and I don't believe he ever spanked or struck me. His anger often centered on food. It was too tough, or it wasn't what he wanted. "I can't eat this crap!" he would yell. "You're the worst cook in the world! Can't you make a simple meal?" Sometimes he would just tip his plate over, but other times he would throw it at the wall, and food and plate shards would fly in all directions.

"I'm sorry, Nels," my mother would say, "I try my best, but we don't have any food in the house."

"Oh, now it's my fault!" he would shout.

"All we have are hot dogs and some boxes of macaroni and cheese. What am I supposed to do? I can't make something from nothing," she would whimper.

"I'm the breadwinner in this family and I need something more substantial. I'm going out to eat!" Then he would leave by the back door and slam it as hard as he could.

These outbursts became part of a Friday ritual. The words changed and the arguments reached different crescendos, but the results were always identical. During the week, he often went directly from work to the bar, and he seldom came home until after dark. On Fridays, he would come home early, take his weekly bath, put on clean clothes, the fireworks would start, and then he would leave. It was common for him to stay away for the entire weekend. In fact, unless he had something special planned for the family, we almost never saw him on weekends. This behavior was, of course, a symptom of some even more destructive behavior going on behind our mother's back, behavior that would eventually break our "happy" little family apart.

CHAPTER 7
A Typical Day

Monotonous is the word that comes to mind when I look back on the fall and winter of 1947. We hibernated inside our little unit, and for me, one particular event pretty much sums it up. My sister and I were sitting at the kitchen table watching our mother clean up the kitchen. "Is it time yet?" I asked as I stared up at the wall clock.

"No, I told you, not until the big hand reaches the top of the circle," Mom answered.

"But it hasn't moved. It's still in the same place."

"Did so!" Jean chimed in.

"Did not!" I shouted.

"What big hand are you talking about, Terry?" Mom asked.

"The big one right there," I said, pointing at the fat hand on the clock.

Mom pointed at the longer of the two hands, "That's the hand I'm talking about—the minute hand. The fat one is the hour hand. No wonder you didn't think it was moving."

"I'm tired of waiting!" I shouted.

"Well, then, *don't* wait. Do something. Go into the living room and play with your toys. I'll call you when the cake is done baking."

Our mother sometimes read nursery rhymes to us, but mostly we played by ourselves. We didn't have playmates, we couldn't go anywhere, and we certainly didn't have TV, CDs, DVDs, or iPods. Television was in its infancy and the rest were a half century away. To compound the problem, Mom was pregnant with our brother Larry, which tended to make her lethargic and, at times, impatient with us. He was born on April 9, 1948, roughly seven months after we left the farm. That tells me the conception must have taken place while we were still living at the farm, which brings up two interesting questions: Did my grandparents know about the pregnancy, and did they ask our mother to leave? I suspect the answer is yes. If we had stayed at the farm, it would have meant another mouth to feed, and my grandparents weren't getting any younger. On top of that, our mother had gone behind their backs and against their wish that she have nothing to do with our father—a wish that I was definitely aware of.

When summer arrived, things improved. At least I could get outside. I loved to ride my tricycle, and according to a relative, I took it very seriously. I would troll up and down the sidewalk in front of our unit for hours at a time in search of cars. When one drove by, I would speed up and, like a dog, try to beat it to the end of the block. I never won, but I had fun trying. When I wasn't doing that, I played with Jean in the sandbox next to the side of our unit and on the swing set. Mostly we played by ourselves, but occasionally Mom would walk us to the park by the community center. Besides a sandbox, the park had a big kids' swing set with a slide at one end, several teeter-totters, and monkey bars. Mom would bring lunch, and we would sit at one of the picnic tables sipping Kool-Aid and eating peanut butter and jelly sandwiches and cookies.

Washday was an exciting adventure. Mom would load my little red wagon with a bundle of dirty clothes, and the three of us would walk the two blocks to the community laundromat. When it was nice out, we would return with the clothes still wet. Mom would pull the wagon to the alley behind our unit and hang the clothes out to dry on one of the umbrella clotheslines in the center of the parking lot while Jean and I chased each other from pole to pole. Because the cement directly under each clothesline had a steep upward slant to it, we would race across the flat parking lot, up the incline, touch the pole, and run back down. One day I asked Mom why the cement around the pole was higher. "I think it's to keep the cars from parking under the clothesline," she replied. "Or," she said, winking at me, "maybe they did it so little boys and girls can run up and down them."

"Yup, that's why," I said, taking off for the nearest pole.

When our father took the time to spend a day or a weekend with us, we would usually go on short trips or to company functions. He once took us on a family excursion to the iron ore docks. The image of large freighters gliding into the loading docks is as clear to me today as it was in 1948. I didn't understand a word he said, but I can still see him pointing at the docks as he explained the loading and unloading process.

The longest trip we took was to the Haataja farm on the outskirts of Menahga, Minnesota. As we drove past a small town called Hubbard, everyone laughed when I asked if this was where Old Mother Hubbard lived. At the Haataja farm, the enormous homemade kitchen table amazed me. Grandma

Haataja, I would later learn, had given birth to sixteen children, of whom thirteen made it past adolescence. That would certainly explain the size of the table.

An employee picnic at the community center that summer goes down as the most exciting time I had at Morgan Park. We watched some of the adults play lawn games, and we ate at a picnic table filled with food, but a clown blowing up and bending balloons into the shape of animals is what sticks in my mind.

"Can I have one? Can I have one?" I pleaded, jumping up and down.

"Of course," the clown said. "What would you like me to make?"

"A dog! Like the one you made for him," I said, pointing at a boy who was walking away.

"Are you sure? I can make all kinds of animals."

"No, I want a dog!"

He blew up a long red balloon for me. I can still hear the squeaking of the latex as he twisted and pulled until I had my wiener dog.

I enjoyed the afternoon at the park, but the real drama of the summer of 1948 involved my father's best friends.

CHAPTER 8
Kicked Out

Alfred and Martha Honkala were my father's best friends and drinking companions. I would meet them on at least four occasions: three while we lived in Morgan Park and once when I turned seven. The first time was at our home. They arrived in the late afternoon on a Saturday. Jean and I watched the couples drinking and talking from the doorway of the upstairs bedroom. After a while, we got tired of watching and listening and climbed back into bed.

The thing that struck me the most is how similar Alfred and Dad were: not in physical stature, because Dad was a good six inches shorter than Alfred, but in the way they conversed with each other. Every other word was a swear word, the accent was unusual and at times incomprehensible, and the discourse had a dueling nature that was loud and overlapping. My mother would later tell me that the funny sing-songy accent was of Finnish origin, and over time, I would intuitively come to understand that the dueling banter was a form of bragging. The cursing was simply Iron Range English 101.

The second encounter happened on a warm late summer afternoon. We were on our way to a carnival when Dad pulled to the curb in front of a bar and said, "I'm going in to get something to take along."

"Will you be gone long?" Mom asked.

"No, no, it'll only take a minute."

He left, and when he opened the door to the bar, a loud burst of country western music and a cacophony of excited voices filled the air. When the door closed, things returned to normal, but off in the distance, I could hear the muffled sound of another kind of music. It was a rhythmic, grinding sound. Looking around, I saw the top of a Ferris wheel above the roof of a building, which meant the carnival was close by. We sat in the car for ten or fifteen minutes, certainly long enough for Dad to get a bottle. Finally Mom said, "I'll go in after him. You kids wait in the car."

We sat in silence for what seemed an eternity—time enough, anyway, for the sweat to start rolling down the side of my face. The trapped heat inside the car was stifling, and it was getting more and more difficult to breathe. When Larry started to squirm and fuss, I said, "I can't stand this." I opened the car door and stepped onto the sidewalk, with Jean following close behind. Then I picked Larry from the car seat we walked into the bar.

It was dark and grimy inside the bar, and smoke hung in the air, making it almost impossible to breathe. At the far end of the bar, a man stood behind a well-lit counter surrounded by people on stools. Behind him were rows of bottles. People sat at tables in the dimly lit center of the room and in booths that ran the full length of the two outer walls. They talked in loud and excited voices. Above the din, I heard my father's voice: "Here's my kids now! Come over here and say 'Hi' to the Honkalas." I spotted him sitting in a booth with our mother. Carrying Larry and holding Jean's hand, I hurried over to the booth.

"How come you didn't come back to the car?" I asked.

Ignoring my question, he said, "You remember Alfred and Martha Honkala, don't you?"

"Of course they remember us," Martha exclaimed. "We were at your house the other day."

"When are we going to go? It's hot!" I whined.

"Well, you came to the right place," Dad said in his loud, obnoxious voice. "Get my kids something to drink," he shouted at the man behind the counter.

"Can't serve children in here, Nels. You know that. You'll have to take them outside!" "The hell you say!" my dad answered. "I can do whatever I please with my kids. Bring them a Coke."

The bartender walked over with two Cokes and said, "Come on, Nels, I don't want any trouble. You can't have those kids in here. After they get done with the drinks they'll have to go outside."

"All right, all right," Dad said, "we'll go as soon as they're done." It was dark when we finally left the bar. Instead of taking us to the carnival, Dad drove us home and Mom put us right to bed. Dad left to meet up with his friends again.

I saw Alfred and Martha one more time that summer. This time, our dad drove us into Duluth to shop for clothes, but instead of going with us, he went straight to a bar. "Come and get me when you're done," he told Mom. "I'll be with Alfred and Martha." After shopping, we killed time by walking on the beach and across the Aerial Lift Bridge. We ended up at the car, which Dad had parked close to the bar. Mom peered inside the bar's front window and then walked back to the car. "Terry, I don't want to go inside. Would you please go in and tell your dad that we're done shopping? I'll stay out here and watch Jean and Larry."

Even at the age of three, I knew what my mother meant. If she went in, he would badger her into staying. We were miles from home and at his mercy. "What do I say?" I asked.

"Tell him we're done shopping and come right back. Don't stay, OK?"

I went into the bar knowing that my father would not come out willingly, and that I would most likely become the target of his anger. When he wasn't drinking, he could charm the pants off anyone, but once he went under the spell of liquor, he became a completely different person. I can honestly say that over my entire lifetime, I have never met anyone quite like my father. He was obnoxious, boisterous, aggressive, foul-mouthed, and always primed for a fight, verbal or otherwise. No child should have to go into a bar for any reason, let alone to tell a father that it is time to leave, but at the age of three, I was already showing signs of becoming my mother's brave little man.

I spotted him right away. He was sitting in a booth across from Alfred and Martha. I put my hands on their table and said, "Mom said it's time to go."

Startled, he looked down at me. "She what? She said it's time to go! Well, who the hell is she to be telling me what to do?" he yelled. "Are you done shopping?"

I nodded. "I got a new pair of pants!"

"You got a new pair of pants," he parroted. "Well, *that's* cause for celebration! Here, sit next to your old man and I'll give you a sip of beer." He slid over and patted the seat next to him.

I shook my head no. "Come on, sit down!" he said, more firmly this time. When I didn't budge, he picked up a salt shaker and sprinkled some salt into his beer. I watched in fascination as the salt settled and bubbles floated to the top of the glass. Then he picked it up and shoved it close to my mouth. "Here, take a little sip. The salt makes it taste better."

"Nels," I heard Martha say, "I don't think you should be doing that."

"Stay out of it, Martha," Alfred said, "a little beer won't hurt him."

"Just one sip," Dad said, shoving the glass closer.

I took one sip. I'm not even sure it was a full sip, but it was enough for me to start gagging. It felt like the insides of my stomach were coming out of my mouth. Dad laughed, and I vaguely remember him saying something about "not being man enough." Then he hit me on the back and they all had a good laugh. Afterwards, as Dad got into the car he said to Mom, "So, now you can't come in yourself, you have to send in your son." He dropped us off at the house and, as before, returned to the bar.

Not long after the incident at the bar, we left Morgan Park under a cloud of shame, triggered by an event that happened one Friday evening during the summer of 1948. After throwing a plate of macaroni and cheese against the wall, followed by his usual curses and belittling comments, my father yelled, "I want you and your brats out of the house! I've had it with your cooking and blathering about not enough this and not enough that!"

"Nels, you don't mean that!" Mom cried. "What will we do, where will we go?"

"I don't give a damn what you do or where you go!" he bellowed. "I'm leaving, and when I return tomorrow morning I don't want to see your ugly face! Do you understand that?"

"Who am I going to call?"

"Call your sister. She hates me. I'm sure she'd love to help you."

"What am I going to put our clothes and other things into? I don't have a suitcase big enough."

"What clothes! What things!" he yelled. "I paid for your clothes and I paid for everything in this house. I don't want you taking anything that I paid for, and that includes the brats' clothes. You can take the clothes on your back and that's it!"

"Nels, you don't mean that…you can't mean that!"

"Don't I? Try me! If I see any of you in the house when I come back tomorrow, I will throw you into the street!" He stormed out the back door, slamming it behind him.

It's almost impossible for me to describe how I felt at that moment. Jean was crying and whimpering, "Don't go, Daddy. Please don't leave us!" I sat frozen to my chair. I felt unwanted and afraid of what would happen to us. Where would we go? Would he really throw us out of the house? I never got an answer to that last question, because Irene and her husband Dan picked us up that night, and we left Morgan Park with the clothes on our backs. The next day, without any forewarning, we were back at the farm with Grandma and Grandpa.

CHAPTER 9
Back in the Nest

The exact date of our return is not clear, but photos dated July 1948 show the four of us at the farm. For Grandma and Grandpa, the sudden return of their daughter, now with three children, must have been a shock—not even a phone call or letter asking if we could move back. Overnight Grandma found herself washing extra clothes, feeding hungry mouths, attending to dirty diapers, and keeping track of two children who were now old enough to disappear in the blink of an eye.

Uncle Alan was happy to see us, but he was not overjoyed with the new sleeping arrangement. After our move to Morgan Park, he had taken over the entire upstairs. With our return, he was forced to squeeze all of his belongings into the smaller bedroom, while we took over the larger one. Jean slept with Mom in a standard-sized bed at one end of the long and narrow room; Larry and I were at the other end. I slept on an Army cot and Larry slept next to me in his crib.

I slept soundly that first night, and when I awoke, Mother

Nature was calling. I raced urgently downstairs and danced on my tiptoes through the dining room and into the kitchen. Grandma spotted me and said, "Well, don't stand there prancing about, Terry, go outside and relieve yourself."

"Do I have to go to the outhouse?"

"From the looks of things, I don't think you're going to make it to the front door," Grandma said. "Besides, you don't have any shoes on. You can go in the dirt by the front door, but don't you dare go on the side of the house." I pushed the screen door open and stepped gingerly onto a wooden plank. Still holding myself, I stepped away, but before I could get things under control, an arc of warm pee showered the siding. "I said in the dirt, not on the house!" Grandma shouted from the kitchen, and I redirected the gusher. "Nels, on your way to the barn would you see if that young rascal needs help?"

"Yesus, leave da boy alone," I heard him reply. "Hell, I'm not going to help him pee and he ain't going to hurt da siding."

He was right, because the siding was the same material as the shingles on the roof. The only difference was color—the siding was green and the roof was red. One section of the house, starting at the center of the upstairs window and extending to the peak of the roof, did not have siding, exposing the house's raw lumber. I can only guess as to the why. Grandpa said the lumberyard ran out of the material, but Alan told me the siding came from a construction site and the local lumberyard never handled the siding.

[Grandpa was a habitual scavenger, so I lean towards Alan's answer. Anyway, I mention the siding because that little unfinished section would later affect my life in a major way.]

As I tucked my privates back into my underwear, Grandpa stepped onto the plank. "How you doing dere, squirt?" he asked. "You got da situation under control den?"

"I'm done. Where are you going?"

"I'm going to da barn to squeeze some juice outta dose heifers," he said, winking at me. "You vanta come along den?"

"You leave the boy here, Grandpa," shouted Grandma from the kitchen. "He's not dressed for the barn. He can stay put until you return if he wants, but I don't want him walking in the dirt."

Grandpa shrugged, winked at me again, and took off, milk pail in hand, down the driveway past the water pump to the barn, which was about sixty yards from the house. In addition to the barn, there were six other utility buildings laid out in a U-shape around the main house: a fishing shack, woodshed, outhouse, pig barn, garage, and bunkhouse. All were unpainted and constructed from weathered, rough-hewn lumber, which blended in with the surrounding trees. With one exception, the buildings did not have siding. Thus they provided little, if any, protection from the elements. The fishing shack was the exception. One of Grandpa's many occupations was fishing guide. He used the shack to store his fishing gear and he kept minnows in a water tank next to the outside wall. To protect his little investment and I say little because from all accounts he didn't make a living at it, Grandpa tacked tarpaper to the lower half of the shack. Why he didn't tarpaper the entire shack is anybody's guess. My guess is that, as he had with the farmhouse, he probably picked the paper up from a construction site and he ran out. I'm sure it didn't do a thing for the minnows during the winter, but I suppose it allowed him to extend the season for a month or two. All of the buildings had shingles. The shingles on the garage and fishing shack were the same as those on the house; the rest had cedar shingles. As for size, the buildings were half the size of those seen on most farms, but the pig barn was by far the smallest. It was the size of a large doghouse.

It didn't take long before things got back to the way they were before—before we became a real family, that is. With the exception of weekends, we seldom saw our mother during the day. My best guess is that she returned to her job in town or at the resort. She certainly wasn't with our father, which had been an on-again, off-again thing during the first two years of my life. When she was home, she helped Grandma with the chores, but she did very little of what you might call mothering. That included discipline. Not long after our return, an incident reestablished Grandma's role as the disciplinarian in the family, and it put an interesting spotlight on one of Grandpa's many traits. After the noon meal, Grandma told everyone that we were going to spend the afternoon at the lake. I put on my swimming suit and climbed into the back seat of the car to wait. At the last minute, Grandma canceled the trip, and I threw a temper tantrum, refusing to get out of the car.

"Grandpa, you get that rascal out of the car and take him to the woodshed," Grandma said, not leaving him any wiggle room.

"Ah, leave the boy alone, he's not going anyplace."

"That young man needs to learn that what I say goes. Take him to the shed and don't you give him one of your lectures, Nels! I want him to feel the rod!"

Grandpa pulled me out of the car and marched me to the shed, with me dragging my feet and sulking the entire way. He lifted me by the shoulders and plopped me onto the chopping block. "Sit and don't move," he said, his accent gone. Taking off his belt, he folded it and knelt down, his eyes level with mine.

Then, snapping the belt several times, he proceeded to give me a lecture. When he finished, he snapped the belt several more times and said, "If we ever have to come to the shed again, this is going to come down hard on your behind, and it'll hurt me just as much as you. Do you understand that?"

"Yes," I whispered, not understanding how the belt would hurt him, but his words and the sincere way he said them made me feel guilty.

"OK! So this is our little secret."

"OK," I said in my best secret-keeping voice. He smiled and gave me a big hug. That was Grandpa, I thought, smiling to myself. He could give a stern lecture, but deep down he was a softy, and I loved him for it.

When Mom was around, she helped around the house, but at Grandma's insistence and to our great relief, she didn't do any of the cooking. Her chores consisted mainly of cleaning, picking up after us, and washing the dishes. Sometimes she would haul wood in from the woodshed or water from the pump that stood in the center of the back yard, but that was rare because Uncle Alan did most of the heavy work.

I pestered Grandma constantly about letting me help, so on days when she wasn't in a hurry, she would let me carry wood or bring in water. I couldn't carry a full pail, so Grandma would fill it part way and I would lug it to the house, walking at an angle with the lip resting against my leg. By the time I got to the house, my legs were always sopping wet and most of the water had soaked into the ground, but I did my best, and it kept me out of mischief.

Making butter was another one of the household chores I pestered Grandma about. I wasn't strong enough to pump the handle of the churn, but Grandma would let me dig the fresh butter out with the paddle—the same paddle she used on my butt, by the way. I would reach into the churn and dig into the soft butter. Then I would pull out a big lump and slap it onto a plate. Grandma would take over when my little arms couldn't reach the bottom.

From time to time Grandma would even let me run errands. One day, she asked me if I would run down to the creek to get some tomatoes, which were stored in jars and dropped into the hole Grandpa dug. I had been down there before but never by myself and never in the evening.

"Terry, would you run down to the creek and fetch me a jar of tomatoes?" Grandma asked as she was preparing the evening meal.

"I'll do it," my mother said, "I don't think Terry's ready for that yet."

"No, I need you here. He knows the way, and I think he can handle it."

"I can do it, Grandma!" I said proudly, excited at the prospect of proving my manhood.

"OK. You run along, and remember, I need a jar of *tomatoes*. You know what they look like, don't you?"

"Uh-huh," I said, and ran out the kitchen door.

I followed the path past the outhouse, through the trees, and down to the creek, which was about a quarter mile from the house. It was dark in the woods, not night-dark, but shadowy-dark, and it was eerily silent. As I went deeper, I began to feel uncomfortable. The hair at the nape of my neck stood up and goose bumps appeared on my arms. I thought about the dangers Grandpa had told me about—the eagles that were strong enough to carry off babies and the bears that could kill you with one swipe of their large paws. Suddenly, I heard the howl of a wolf. Startled, I rushed to the creek, grabbed a string, and pulled out a jar. Then, without checking to see what was in it, I turned and ran back up the path, my little legs churning as fast as they would go, my heart racing wildly. I didn't stop until I reached the house. I was out of breath and shell-shocked by stress. It wasn't until I handed the jar to Grandma that I realized my mistake. "Those aren't tomatoes, those are green beans!" Grandma said. After I explained what happened, Grandma said, "That's OK. We'll have green beans for supper tonight, and tomorrow we'll have tomatoes."

On the weekends, Mom would sometimes take us for walks. One day, after we had gone only a short distance, I stopped to tie my shoe, and when I looked up, a bear and her cub were crossing the road in front of us. Wolf, Grandpa's dog, barked and ran after the bears. Mom turned the stroller around and said, "Come kids, let's get back to the house."

"What's going to happen to Wolf?" I asked as I watched the bears lumber into the woods, with Wolf close behind.

"He'll be fine. Come on, Terry." That ended our little walk, but Wolf didn't return for two days. When he did, he walked with a slight limp, one of his ears was tattered and torn, burrs were sticking to his fur, and patches of fur were missing. When I called for him, he ignored me and went straight to his bowl, which Grandma had filled with food.

Washdays were always busy. I don't know why, but Grandma insisted on doing all the washing. At least, I don't recall ever seeing Mom do it. The washing machine stood in the dirt behind the doghouse. I have a mental picture of Grandma standing over the tub, her hair uncombed, sweat streaming down her face, rubbing a pair of pants or a sheet against the washboard. When they were clean, she would run them through the two rollers atop the machine. As she turned the crank, the clothes would come out as flat as a pancake. Grandma would shake them, spraying water in all directions, and hang them on the clothesline that stretched from the side of the house to the birch trees at the edge of the woods. This routine continued throughout the year. During prolonged periods of rough winter weather, Grandma might wash a pair of pants or a dress in the kitchen sink, but on clear winter days, it wasn't unusual to see her in the back yard up to her elbows in suds. The clothes froze almost as soon as Grandma hung them up, and when she took them down, I was often at her side. I enjoyed the fresh smell, and I loved to press my hand into the frozen fabric, watching with amazement the impression it left. I can still hear Grandma shout, "Terry, get your dirty hands off my clean sheets!" but I couldn't help myself any more than people who reach out and touch a door or a wall next to a "wet paint" sign.

Winter was not my favorite time of year. For someone my age there wasn't much to do outside, and with no insulation, there were areas within the house that were freezing cold. To stay warm, we would gather around the table in the kitchen, play with our toys, and take in the aroma of Grandma's baking. After supper, we would play cards or board games by the potbellied stove in the dining room. Sometimes Mom would read to us or we would listen to one of Grandpa's stories. When it was time for bed, we would brush our teeth at the kitchen sink, Grandpa would light a lantern for us, and after we said our goodnights, Mom would lead us up upstairs.

Despite the farm's bucolic isolation and the shoddy appearance of the buildings, it was home, and I was excited to be back. I had never completely taken to city life—the streets lined with houses, the noises of cars and trucks as they sped down busy streets and highways, the boring days spent indoors with nothing to do, and the smell of hot dogs and macaroni and cheese. The sounds and smells of the farm were familiar and reassuring. I loved to hear Grandma's chatter. I enjoyed the smell of freshly baked bread, rolls, and pies. I had missed the sound of the wind whistling through the trees, the high-pitched noises of grasshoppers as they rubbed their hind legs together, the chirping of birds and the chatter of squirrels, and in the evening, the occasional howl of a wolf or the hoot of an owl. I was back in my own little world, my comfort zone.

CHAPTER 10
Breaking the Rules

In late spring 1949 I fell off the pig barn, breaking my collarbone. It all started the morning Jean and I went to the cow pasture with Grandma to help her pick wild mushrooms. The dew was still on the grass and a low mist hung over the pasture. As we followed her around, being careful not to step in cow pies, Grandma talked about the difference between good and bad mushrooms. "Some mushrooms are poisonous. You can die from eating them. That's why it's important to know the difference between good and bad ones."

"How do you know?" I asked.

"Because, when I was a little girl, I watched my mom pick mushrooms, and I've been doing it ever since." She bent over and tilted the head of one. "This mushroom isn't the right color, it doesn't have gills, and when I pinch it like this, it doesn't turn purple. That means it's not good to eat."

I nodded, but I was still confused. To me, the mushroom looked the same as the one she had just put into her basket. "Is this a good one?" I asked, running over to a mushroom that looked like something I'd seen in a comic book.

"No, that's a poisonous one," she said. I jerked my hand back, not sure if it would kill me, and for the rest of the morning I followed Grandma without saying a word. After we returned to the house, Jean and I stayed outside to play. At mealtime, Grandma called us in. On my plate were green beans and a small steak with mashed potatoes and gravy. In the gravy were bits of what looked like small pieces of meat. I stuck my fork into one of them, and feeling no resistance, I asked, "Grandma, what's this?"

"Those are the mushrooms you helped pick," she replied.

[Now I should say that unlike in some homes, where children get to choose what and how much they want to eat, at Grandma and Grandpa's we ate what was on our plate. If we didn't, we had to sit at the table until it was gone, and there were no exceptions to that rule. I know, because I had the pleasure of sitting at the table for over an hour once, staring at a plate full of liver and onions. I hated the taste of liver, and onions didn't particularly appeal to me either. When I finally realized the futility of my stubbornness, I cut the liver into small pieces and, getting the dry heaves with every bite, I swallowed the chunks whole, until the plate was clean.]

Shoving the mushrooms aside, I ate everything else on my plate. Then, staring at the dark brown slimy pieces swimming in what was left of the gravy, I considered the seriousness of the matter. This was a life and death situation, I thought. I was sure I had seen Grandma pick up mushrooms that she had told me were poisonous. But what could I do? I had to clean my plate, so I pointed at my food and said, "I don't want to eat that."

"You know the rules," said Grandma. "Eat everything on

your plate, and that includes the mushrooms. When you're done eating, you can go out to play. Try them, you'll like them. See?" she said, putting several into her mouth. "They taste good!"

"No!" I shouted. Pushing myself away from the table, I ran out the door, and I didn't stop until I got to the pig barn, which was like an oversized doghouse with a fenced-in yard for the mother pig and her babies. When the mother pig saw me, she grunted and moved toward me, with the babies following close behind.

"Terry, get in the house, right now!" Grandma shouted. I could tell by the tone of her voice as she walked toward me that she was serious, but I was already climbing onto the fence. Then, for reasons I have never understood, I pulled myself onto the roof of the pig barn and stood with my feet planted on each side of the peak, my hands on my hips, my lips held tightly together. "Terry, get down from the roof right now!"

"No! I hate you and your dumb food!"

"Get down before you get hurt!" Grandma yelled, reaching out to grab me. I moved to avoid her hands, and as I did, the heel of my shoe caught on a nail sticking out of the roof. I fell headfirst onto the back of the mother pig and from there into the soupy mixture of mud and manure that served as her little piece of this world. What happened next is fuzzy. I recall someone shouting, "Sooee, sooee," and arms lifting me out of the sloppy mess, but most of all I remember a dull, throbbing pain and my left arm dangling uselessly at my side.

Doctor Heim put my arm in a sling and told me that when the bone healed it would be thicker and stronger than it had been before the accident. It's funny how little things like that stick in the mind of a young boy. I very distinctly remember the feeling of pride that swelled in me, and I recall thinking, "Wow, my collarbone will be better than other people's!"

CHAPTER 11
The Great Bed

It was midnight when we returned home from the hospital. Grandma told Mom that I could sleep with her and Grandpa in the Great Bed. Despite the discomfort and the nuisance of having my arm in a sling, the invitation perked me up.

No one knew where the name came from, but Grandpa was proud of his bed. "Well, it's time to visit the Great Bed," he would say, or "You can stay up as long as you wish, but it's time for us to greet the Great Bed." Once I asked him why he called it that, and he said, "Well, I'm not sure, but my parents always called it the Great Bed, and we kept up the tradition." Maybe it was because the bed belonged to someone great once, an important ancestor perhaps, or maybe it was the bed's bulk. Solid oak and stained dark brown, it took up seventy-five percent of the space in the bedroom. Thick, square corner posts with balls affixed to their tops stretched up to the ceiling, and the headboard and footboard were almost identical in height. That, and the bed's thick sideboards, gave me the impression that Grandpa had built the house around the bed. He told me it came from Norway, just like the wooden skis that hung on the wall in the woodshed. The only other furniture in the room was a massive upright dresser and a tall chest that Grandpa laughingly called his Butler's Closet. When I asked him why he called it that, he said, "Because it takes care of my clothes." I remember thinking his words did not make sense. Closets do not take care of clothes—Grandma did that.

With the sleeping arrangement settled, Mom helped me into my pajamas. Then, holding a lantern in front of her, she disappeared upstairs, and Grandma and Grandpa led me into the master bedroom. Being careful of my injury, Grandpa laid me as close to the center of the Great Bed as he could. To my astonishment, I sank deep into the heart of the mattress, and for an instant, I panicked. It was the same feeling I had had when Grandpa first taught me to float in the lake. I grabbed with my good arm for the sheet, but this did not stop me from sinking. When I came to a stop, the top of the mattress was above my head. To my great relief, I could still breathe. "Grandpa, how come the mattress is so soft?" I asked.

"Dat's because it's stuffed vit goose fedders," he said. "Not da big fedders you see lying in da grass, but doze fluffy vuns – da vuns dat float in da air." He went on to explain that it took months and months to gather enough feathers for a bed, and he concluded, "City folks couldn't buy a mattress like dis, even if dey vanted to." Evidently Grandpa's feather mattress was rare, I thought, and I speculated that Grandpa had gathered the feathers and stuffed the mattress himself. "Move up a little and slide more towards da middle so Grandma and I can get in," said Grandpa as he snuffed out the last lantern. I pushed with my feet and grabbed the mattress cover to help me move to the center of the bed. Grandpa wore his dark plaid pajamas and Grandma wore an ankle-length, rose-colored nightgown. When Grandpa landed in the bed, his weight almost lifted me off the sheets. I didn't fly into the air when Grandma crawled in, but afterwards I felt as if I was lying on top of a giant marshmallow.

"You won't squish me, will you?" I asked, dreading the thought of what might happen if I slid off my perch and rolled under one of them in the middle of the night.

"Well, if you're going to roll, roll in my direction," said Grandma. "Your Grandpa doesn't know what's going on once he falls asleep."

Grandma's words were not encouraging. To play it safe, I scooted closer to her. "What if I have to go potty?" I whispered.

"You just say 'I need to go potty,' and I'll help you," answered Grandma.

A deep silence fell over the house. I lay there in the comfort of the Great Bed listening to the tick-tock of the grandfather clock in the living room. Off in the distance I heard the hoot of an owl, but before Grandpa could let out his first snort, sleep overtook me.

CHAPTER 12
Someone Else's Brats

I have no memory of the day we left the farm for the second time, and I have been unable to find a specific date. As for the why, Grandma told our mother she could no longer care for us. After all, she was cooking and cleaning for seven people, and that's not an easy task for anyone, let alone a woman in her fifties who didn't have any modern conveniences.

We moved in with Aunt Irene, her husband Dan, and their young son, who was Jean's age. How long we stayed with them is also unknown, but I suspect it didn't last long, because I have no memories of the sleeping arrangements, of Irene's cooking, or of playtime activities. I found one photo of their son and me sitting outside on our tricycles, but it didn't bring back any memories, which is, I think, another sign that our stay was short. The memories I do have are mainly of Uncle Dan, and I know one of them is from April 1, 1950, because it was the first time anyone pulled an April Fool's joke on me. The joke was short and simple and I can almost see the words, but they fail me. The recollection I have is one of humiliation. When Dan laughed at his little prank, he made me feel like a dummy for believing him. Aunt Irene told Dan that it wasn't funny, and she scolded him for picking on a little boy.

From the start, Uncle Dan complained about our presence. He had a booming voice, and he could be obnoxious at times. One day he said something that I've never forgotten. I was playing in the living room and the adults were in the kitchen talking. I could hear bits and pieces of their conversation, but nothing was intelligible until Dan suddenly exclaimed, "I'm not going to raise someone else's brats!" This was followed by something about "putting them in a home with the other brats."

A day or two later, our mother gathered us in the living room. At first, she struggled with her words, often choking and stopping, as if trying to gather her thoughts. She told us that a caseworker would stop by later in the morning to pick us up. We would go for a ride with this person to a home where we would stay for a few days with other children our age while she found a job and a place to live.

"Will it be our new home?" I asked, thinking she meant we would all be together.

"No, it's just temporary," she answered. "It's a place you children can stay until I make other arrangements." She tried her best to sound positive, but something in the tone of her voice betrayed her. I had a strange feeling in the pit of my stomach that things weren't right.

After she bathed and dressed us, she shooed us out onto the screened-in porch to await the arrival of the caseworker. Around ten o'clock a black four-door sedan pulled up in front of the house. A tall, plain-looking woman with dark brown hair and bright red lipstick got out. She walked around to our side of the car, opened the rear door, and then she just stood there, frozen to the spot, as if she was guarding something. She wore a black hat with a veil and a black wool overcoat that hung past her knees. It was a good thing she was standing on the grass, I thought. With all that black, if she had stood on the street next to the car I wouldn't have been able to see her. Jean yelled, "Mom, she's here."

"OK, I'll be right there. Tell your brothers to get ready."

I didn't know what she meant by "get ready." As far as I knew, she hadn't packed a suitcase. The only things we had to worry about were the clothes on our backs. Soon our mother walked onto the porch with Aunt Irene and her son. She was *not* carrying a suitcase. "Good luck, Eileen," I heard Irene say. "I'm sorry about Dan. I hope things turn out for you and the kids."

"Thank you. I hope so too," our mother said as she herded us out the screen door. The woman introduced herself as Mrs. Severson, and we all climbed into the car. Our mother sat in the front seat and the three of us sat in the rear. As Mrs. Severson drove, I rubbed the dark brown material on the armrest. It moved back and forth just like the material in Grandpa's car did. It even had the same smell. "Why does it smell funny?" I asked.

"What smell?" asked Mrs. Severson.

"It smells like Grandpa's barn."

"Oh," she chuckled, "that's because I live on a farm and the garage is attached to the barn. I guess I'm used to it."

"Where are we going?"

"We're going to a place where there are lots of other children your age," our mother cut in, "and you're going to be staying there for a few weeks."

"You said we'd be staying a few *days*," I said, glaring at her.

"It'll just be for a *short* time," she said.

"What's a short time?" I asked, squirming in my seat and not wanting to hear anything beyond a few days. I didn't know how to tell time, but I knew the difference between a few days and a few weeks.

She tried her best to make me believe this was only a temporary arrangement. "I'll see you on weekends, and before you know it we'll be living together again." I didn't know what to make of this. What did she mean by "I'll see you on weekends?" What did seeing us on weekends have to do with staying with other children for a few days or even weeks?

Homes and businesses flew by as the car sped across town. As we passed through the downtown commercial district of Duluth, I looked out the car's window and stared in wonder at the throngs of people crowding the sidewalks. Why were they in such a hurry, I thought, and what were they doing at this time of the day? We left the business district and entered a residential area. A few blocks later, Mrs. Severson slowed the car and made a left turn. The car climbed a steep hill and when the hill leveled out, she came to a stop. Well, we're here," she said. By *here*, I gathered she was referring to the five-story, yellow brick building off to our right. The only other buildings in the vicinity were residential homes and none of them were anywhere near the car. I searched for signs of life, but seeing none, I studied the architecture of the building. It was unlike anything I had ever seen before. The roof sloped like any residential home, with one exception. This roof had a secondary slope, and sticking out of it were five little houses. Each had its own window, and the middle one, which was bigger and higher up in elevation, had an arched window. Shifting my focus to ground level, I noticed that a wide cement staircase rose steeply to the first floor of what looked like a two-story three-season porch or veranda. In the center was a set of double screen doors that served as the main entrance. Four pillars on the exterior of the wood and glass structure gave it a unique Romanesque look, and between the pillars were windows. At the very top, I saw some bold letters covering the entire width of the veranda's facing. "What does that say?" I asked.

"The Children's Home," said my mother. Mrs. Severson mumbled, "I guess they could have chosen a more creative name."

"Where are the children?" I asked.

"It's noon. I imagine they are in the dining room eating right now," the caseworker replied. We sat there for a few minutes, staring at the building, not saying anything and not wanting to get out of the car. Finally, she said, "Do you want to see the neighborhood?"

"Yes, of course, that would be nice," answered our mother.

"Some of the older children play on the city lot over there," Mrs. Severson said, pointing across the street at a flat open area about the size of a city block. The surface of the area was sun-baked yellow clay. Here and there, a few tufts of grass sprouted out of the ground, but overall it looked like the schoolyard in Morgan Park, minus the playground trappings. "Chester Creek is behind those trees on the far side of the lot," she continued. "We don't allow the children to go down by the creek without supervision, but the swings and slides up there on the ridge," she said, pointing at an area at the far end of the lot, "are available for the children who are old enough to cross the street by themselves."

"Is the playground a part of the home?" our mother asked.

"No, I think it belongs to the city. The houses in the area were built around the turn of the century for dock workers and their families. That one on the other side of the parking lot is the girls' cottage, where the older girls stay."

"What age are they?" my mother asked.

"I think it's either seven or eight. If you want, I'll find out for you, but I don't believe Jean's old enough yet."

"No, that's OK," replied my mother.

The houses on our tour all looked the same to me—two-story structures with three-season porches. Some were two-tone rust and a few were different shades of brown or gray, but most were white. Packed tightly together at exactly the same distance from the curb, they reminded me of toy soldiers lined up for battle. The only thing different about the girls' cottage was its oversized dormer with a picture window that overlooked the parking lot. Mrs. Severson, continuing the tour commentary, said, "Over there is the old water reservoir." Looking in the direction she was pointing, I saw a large cement wall about nine feet high rising out of a steep grassy incline. The top was flat, and from my viewpoint, it took up the entire block. "It's out of use now," she said, "but I understand that at one time it was considered the largest water reservoir ever built."

"Can you walk on it?" I asked.

"No!" Mrs. Severson said. "The children are not allowed up there. It's too dangerous. Someone might fall through and get hurt." She drove past more of the same houses, made two more turns, and came to a stop on the east side of the Home—the side overlooking the harbor. "Not much of a tour, I know, but at least you have a better feel for the neighborhood."

"Yes. Thank you," our mother said. "That was a nice tour." I took Jean's and Larry's hands. When we were about halfway up the steep entrance steps, I let go and sat sulking with my arms folded over my chest. Mom grabbed me by the arm and half carried, half dragged me the rest of the way. At the large double doors, she bent over, grabbed me by the shoulders, and said, "What will the other children think when they see you acting like this?"

I looked at her with clenched teeth and said, "I don't care what they think. I'm not going to stay here, and you can't make me!"

"Oh, Terry, I was hoping we wouldn't have to go through this," she pleaded. "This is one of those times when I need you to be my brave little man. Can you do that for me?"

"No, I don't *want* to be a man," I hissed. "I'm *not* a man, I'm just a little boy, and you can't make me!" Mrs. Severson opened the door and stood to the side as our mother marshaled us into our new home.

"Always a fun center, the piano here serves as the backdrop for a story hour, with Superintendent Floy E. Scheidler presiding." **Duluth News Tribune**, Nov. 23, 1947

CHAPTER 13
The Home

April 1950, Duluth, Minnesota. The dark-stained oak flooring of the Children's Home made an eerie echo sound as our hard-soled shoes hit its worn surface. Mom, her unbuttoned coat exposing a plain print cotton dress, pushed Jean and Larry ahead of her with her right hand while she held my arm with her left. Half lifting me, she pulled me down a narrow passageway and into a high-ceilinged lobby that looked bigger than Grandma and Grandpa's farmhouse. From an archway cut into the center of the inside wall, I heard children's voices and the clatter of forks and spoons hitting plates, and I smelled the aroma of food. Mrs. Severson bent over and pointed at a miniature church pew parked against the wall. "Do you think you could sit over there and be nice and quiet while your mother and I go into the office?"

"No, I want to go with my mom," I whimpered.

"Your mom and I will be gone for a short time. We're going into the office," she said,

"What office?" I snapped. Would our mother leave without saying goodbye? Would she disappear and never come back?

"The door to the office is around the corner, just to the left of the front entrance," she said, pointing at the two big glass doors.

Knowing my proclivity for acting out, Mom took action. She grabbed me by the arms, lifted me off the ground, and sat me hard on the pew. Jean and Larry followed without a fuss. "I'll be back in a few minutes," she said firmly, crouching down to our level. "I want you to sit still and behave yourself. Jean, you hold Terry's hand. Make sure he stays put."

Mom and the woman went into the office and we sat in silence, listening to the noises of the children. It didn't take long before Larry started to squirm. Leaning his back against Jean and using the armrest for leverage, he pushed Jean tightly against me with his legs. I pushed on Jean in an effort to get him back to his corner of the bench, "Would you stop moving around?" I said. I was wound up. My pulse was beating rapidly and my nerves were ready to explode as I gripped the armrest.

Suddenly, one of the children from the dining room poked his head around the corner of the archway. He stared at us for a few seconds, and then he let out a squeal and hid behind the door. I heard an adult voice say, "Steven, stop gawking and get back to your table."

When the same boy reappeared a few minutes later, a fork in one hand and a thumb in his mouth, I snapped, "What are you staring at? Go away!" He spun on the balls of his feet and darted back into the dining room.

"Steve," the same adult voice shouted, "I thought I told you to sit down. Stop bothering those children."

For a moment, there was complete silence, followed by a

low murmur. Then someone shouted, "Yeah, Steve sit down," which was followed by an uproar, laughter, and more chatter.

The minutes dragged. Eventually the tension in my body subsided and I began to process my surroundings. With the exception of our pew, the room was bare. High dark-stained oak baseboards, thick doorframes, and hardwood floors overpowered dull, cream-colored plastered walls, which had dozens of thin spider cracks spreading out from both top and bottom. A steam radiator painted the same dull cream stood against the wall and an immense glass chandelier hung over the bare floor. Light from enormous windows streamed down wide staircases on either side of the room and from the heavy glass entrance doors. The ornately etched glass edges of the doors, like the chandelier, seemed out of place with the rest of the interior.

Finally, the sounds coming from the room behind us and the smell of food got the best of me. I pulled my hand out of my sister's grip and slid down from the bench. "Terry, Mom said you should stay," Jean said, in that reprimanding way that was so like Grandma's. Ignoring her, I walked toward the children's voices and peered around the corner of the archway. I was prepared to see children eating, but their sheer numbers startled me. I had never seen that many boys and girls sitting in one place in my entire life. There had to be seventy-five of them, and they were all sitting, standing, or kneeling on wooden chairs in front of at least six tables. One boy was standing on his chair reaching for a chicken leg from one of many large bowls sitting in the center of the table. Instead of plates, the children were eating on rectangular silvery trays with ridges on the inside. Adults were eating at two tables in the front of the room. Their tables were arranged perpendicular to the children's tables, giving them a full view of everything that was taking place in the room. In the space that divided this seating arrangement were three highchairs. The chairs were facing the children, and the middle one, I noticed, was almost twice the size of the other two. In it sat a boy about my age wearing a black cone-shaped paper hat. Babies occupied the other two.

The room became silent when the children sensed my presence. They all turned as if on cue and stared back at me. Several of them said something I couldn't make out and then, just as suddenly as the noises had ended, the clamor of excited voices and the clink of metal started up again.

"Terry," boomed my mother's voice, "I thought I told you to stay seated on the bench." Startled, I turned to see her walking toward me with a woman I had never seen before. At the same time, Jean slid from the bench and grabbed the arm of Larry, who was standing in the middle of the room. "I have someone I want you to meet," Mom said. "This is the superintendent, Mrs. Scheidler." Panic, or something close to it, struck me as I looked up at one of the scariest faces I'd ever seen. She was a thin, unattractive woman with fluffy, short, mouse-brown hair, a high forehead, a tapered, egg-shaped face, thin lips, and a sharp pointed nose upon which sat a pair of round glasses. Her features, along with the black, sleeveless dress she was wearing, made her look like the Wicked Witch of the West. The only thing missing was a pointed hat and a wart at the end of her nose.

"Hi, children," the Witch said, "I've heard so many good things about you from your mother. Would you please come into my office? I'd like to get to know you better." Looking over her shoulder, she asked, "Do you want something to drink? Milk and a cookie maybe?" We all shook our heads no. The social worker who had driven us to the Children's Home glanced up from behind a desk as we walked past her towards what I assumed was the Witch's office. The first thing I noticed as we entered her office was the color. Instead of a dull cream, the walls were painted mint green, giving off a cheery and warm feeling. The room was flooded with light from a large arched window. This stood in sharp contrast to its main occupant—a contrast, I might add, that would prove to be prophetic.

Come in and have a seat," the Witch said. "I'll bet you're exhausted from your trip and from the newness of the situation." We stood in the middle of the room, frozen by fear. "Please don't be frightened," she continued. "I won't hurt you. I want to help your mother and give you a place to stay until she can get a job and find a new home for you. I'm sure it won't be long, and meanwhile you'll have lots of other children to play with." She gently placed her hand on my shoulder, but I immediately brushed it aside.

"I don't want to be here!" I shrieked.

The Witch looked at Mom and said, "I think you better go now. I'll deal with this."

Mom put her hand to her mouth as tears started rolling down her cheeks. "I'm sorry, children," she murmured. "I promise I'll come every weekend. We'll have lots of fun and. . ."

The words stuck in her throat. She knelt to hug us and we put our arms around her neck, crying. "Mom, don't go. Don't leave us here," we pleaded, each in our own way.

"I'm not leaving you. I promise! I'll visit you all the time, and before you know it, we'll be a family again," she kept saying, until at last I felt the hands of Mrs. Scheidler and the caseworker pulling us apart. One of them held me in a firm grip, and as I fought to get free, Mom rose from the floor and turned away.

"I hate you! I never want to see you again!" I screamed as she walked out the door, leaving us in the care of complete strangers.

CHAPTER 14

Checking for Head Lice

An old beekeeper once told me that bees, when trapped inside a building, are harmless because they become disoriented. After my mother left, I became submissive. It was as if, like the bees, my navigational guidance system had become completely disabled. Stinging the keepers was the furthest thing from my mind. I did what I was told, and I followed orders without putting up a fuss.

The rest of that first day at the Children's Home passed quickly. Instead of eating in the dining room like the other children, a matron escorted us to the kitchen, and we ate with the cooks, who fussed over us as if we were new hatchlings. Afterwards, another matron took us to see the head nurse, Miss Lind, who had a nursing station on the second floor with an examination table, a desk, and a medicine cabinet. Shortly after we stepped into her waiting room, she came out and introduced herself. She was plain looking, of medium height and weight, with wavy, mouse-brown hair, gray eyes, and bright red lipstick. I remember the lipstick and the hair because everything else, from the cap on her head to her nylons and shoes, was white. Her cap's Red Cross emblem was in the left corner rather than the center. For some reason, this little detail captured my attention.

Miss Lind took Larry into the examining room first, followed by Jean. When she called me in, I noticed that another door to the examination room was open to the hallway, and not seeing either my brother or sister, I got anxious and asked, "Where are Jean and Larry?"

"I'm sorry. They're with Miss Kelly," she said as she closed the door to the hallway. "She's in charge of the nursery and the supervisor of the second floor, but since you're a big boy, you'll be staying on the third floor."

"How come I can't see them? My mom said I'm supposed to watch them."

"You can see them later. Meanwhile, I want to get to know you better." She asked me a whole bunch of questions. She wanted to know when I was born, where I had lived before, what my parents' names were, what my favorite foods were, and best of all, she wanted to know if I had any pets. I told her about my dog Wolf and answered her questions as best as I could. She checked my eyes and ears and put something cold on my chest, saying that she wanted to listen to my heart. After that, she dug her sharp fingernails into my scalp until it hurt and said, "Very nice, Terry, you have thick hair. I wish I had your hair." Then she asked me to take off my clothes. At first I refused, but when she told me I didn't have to take my underwear off, I gave in and stripped to my shorts. She checked my feet and arms, hit my knees with a rubber hammer, and wrote something down on a clipboard.

"What are you doing?" I asked.

"I'm writing that you're very healthy. You can put your clothes back on, and when Miss Dettborn gets here, she'll escort you to the third floor."

"Who is that?"

"Miss Dettborn is one of the matrons on the third floor and she'll help you get settled in."

As if on cue, a woman poked her head in the door and asked, "Done?"

"He's yours," said Miss Lind. "Terry, this is Miss Dettborn. She'll take it from here."

"OK, follow me, young man. We're going to have some fun." Miss Dettborn was a large woman, not tall, but heavy, with a round pink face and short chubby arms. Her gray hair, braided in a circle on the top of her head, gave her a grandmotherly look. "How would you like to take a bath in a special tub?" she asked.

"How come it's special?"

"You'll see."

She took me to the bathroom on the third floor, and as soon as we walked in, I understood what she meant. The entire right side of the room was a miniature version of a Roman bath, complete with artwork shimmering up from the bottom of the pool and black and white tile everywhere. When Miss Dettborn asked me to take off my clothes, I did not hesitate. In fact, she was still saying something about "getting my clothes washed by tomorrow" and "my mother not bringing a change of clothes" as I slithered down the steps. The water was warm and soapy and soon up to my chest. For the first time since my arrival, I relaxed. "This is fun!" I said, jumping up and down. "Do I get to take a bath every day?"

"Bath time is every Saturday night, but you can only stay in for a short time. The other boys have to use the pool too. Come over here. I'll wash you and then you can go back to playing."

"Does everyone take a bath together?"

"Not everyone can fit at one time, but if we did it one at a time, we'd be here all day."

"How many come in?"

"Oh, six or seven, it depends. I'll let you stay longer this time because it's your first day, but in the future you will need to wash and get out quickly." She washed my hair and scrubbed me until my skin was pink. Then I jumped back in to rinse the soap off, and she let me splash around for a few more minutes. Afterwards, she dried me with a towel and slipped a nightshirt over my head. It was starched and spotless, and I felt clean and refreshed.

CHAPTER 15
The Boys' Dorm

Holding my hand, Miss Dettborn escorted me down the wide third-floor hallway that ran from one end of the building to the other until we came to a set of swinging doors. She pushed on them and we stepped into a large room. Inside were at least twenty twin-sized beds lined up on either side of a center aisle. "I think we'll give you a bed somewhere around the center. How about this one?" It wasn't really a question; she was just trying to be nice, and I knew it, so I didn't say anything. She unrolled the mattress until it landed with a plop. Then she said, "I need to get some sheets and a blanket. Will you be OK by yourself?"

"Uh-huh," I nodded. I looked around, wondering what to make of the other boys. They all seemed bigger and older. Several were already in bed, but most were horsing around. Two boys at the far end of the room were standing outside the window. "What are they standing on?" I asked a boy who was walking by.

"That's the fire escape, dummy," he snickered. "Haven't you ever seen a fire escape before?"

"Yes," I lied, not wanting to show my ignorance. "Can I go on it?"

"No, you're not supposed to."

"How come those boys do?"

"Steven, Jimmy, get off of the fire escape!" I heard Miss Dettborn yell from somewhere behind me. "You know you're not supposed to be out there." The two boys quickly climbed back into the room and closed the window.

"Terry, can you help me make the bed?" Miss Dettborn asked, throwing the sheets on the mattress and tossing what looked like one of Grandpa's old Army blankets and a pillow onto a wooden chest at the foot of the bed.

"What's that?" I asked, pointing at the chest.

"That's for your clothes and your valuables."

"What do you mean, my...what did you call them?"

"Valuables—money, or things you don't want someone to see. No, I shouldn't say that. If you have any money, it's better if you let us keep it in the safe instead of in the chest, but other things like...well, things that belong to you."

"Does it lock?"

"No, but like I said, if you have something that's really valuable, we'll keep it in the safe for you...OK?"

"All right," I shrugged.

After we made the bed and she tucked me in, Miss Dettborn asked me if I wanted to say my prayers. She hadn't asked any of the other children if they wanted to say their prayers, and I didn't want to be the only one praying, so I said, "No."

"All right, quiet down, boys," she said, clapping her hands. "It's time to turn the lights out. I do not want to hear any talking after I leave. Is that understood?"

"Yes, Miss Dettborn," several of the boys said in unison. She switched off the lights and the room turned instantly silent as if the switch was somehow connected to the vocal cords of each boy. A yellowish glow from under the doors and from the streetlights silhouetted the beds, but the face of the boy next to me was unrecognizable. I lay awake, tossing and turning, listening to the distant, muffled sounds of the city, the squeaking of beds, and an occasional cough. Gradually, the urge to use the bathroom swept over me. I knew I should get up, but I wasn't sure if I could find the bathroom, and despite the lights in the hallway, I was afraid of what lay beyond the doors. At last, I felt the warmth of my urine seeping through my nightclothes and onto the mattress. It felt comforting somehow, like when I slept next to my mother. Finally, I fell into a deep sleep.

I awoke the next morning to the noises of children and a woman's voice shouting, "Time to rise and shine!" The lights went on, followed by the thumps of tiny feet hitting the hard wood floor. Peeking out from under my blanket, I saw some boys still in their nightshirts and others partially dressed. A few early birds were already fully clothed and on their way out the door. I started to pull my covers off, but when the realization of what I had done during the night hit me, I froze in terror. I felt the cold wetness of the bed and smelled the strong acidy odor of urine. Pulling the sheets up to my chin, I lay there, not daring to move. I couldn't—the other boys would see me. I was petrified. I couldn't remember the last time I had wet the bed. After all the other boys were gone, the woman walked over to my bed. "You're the new boy, aren't you?" she asked, her hands on her hips. "What's your name?" Tall and large boned, she spoke in a way that said she wasn't someone you wanted to mess with. Except for her size, she reminded me of Grandma.

"Terry," I mumbled, pulling the sheets tighter to my chin.

"I'm Miss Knutson, the supervisor on this floor," she said with some authority. "I live here, so you'll be seeing a lot of me." She paused, waiting for me to respond. Not hearing anything, she asked, "Are you OK? You're not sick, are you?"

I didn't answer. Instead, I turned away from her gaze and pulled the covers off, revealing a large yellow stain on what had been clean white sheets the night before. "Oh, my," she said. "That won't do! Is that the first time you've wet your bed, honey?" I nodded yes, my head bowed, my eyes staring at nothing in particular. "OK, don't worry about it, but tonight we'll put a pad on your bed, just to be safe."

"I won't do it again," I stammered as I swung my legs out of bed. "I promise."

"We'll see. If you don't wet the bed again, we'll take the pad off." She cleaned me up, gave me fresh clothes to wear, and escorted me downstairs to breakfast.

CHAPTER 16

The Nursery

By the time Mrs. Knutson and I arrived in the dining room, most of the children had already eaten and gone. I watched as one of the few who remained picked up a brown paper bag from a table as she walked out of the room, "What's in the bag?" I asked.

"That's her school lunch," she replied. "When you're big enough to go to school, you'll get a bag too."

I looked around the room expecting to see Jean and Larry, but they were nowhere in sight. "Where are my sister and brother?"

"I'm sure they're upstairs in the nursery by now. I'll take you up there after we get done eating."

We sat at one of the empty tables, and for the most part, we ate in silence. Mrs. Knutson was OK, I thought. She hadn't scolded me about wetting the bed, and despite her directness, she seemed genuinely concerned about my welfare. She wasn't particularly pretty, not in a stylish way. She didn't wear lipstick or makeup and her hair was curly and cut short, but she was pleasing to look at.

After we finished eating, Mrs. Knutson escorted me out of the dining room. "How old are your sister and brother?" she asked as we walked up the steps to the second floor.

"My sister is three and my brother is two," I replied, trying my best to keep up with her.

"You're the *big* brother. I'll bet they'll be excited to see you."

"Where did they sleep?"

"They slept in one of the dorms on the second floor," she said as we made the first landing. "This is where the babies and the toddlers sleep, but you're a big boy. That's why *you* get to sleep on the third floor."

"How come there aren't any girls on the third floor?"

"Because when the girls get to be your age they move over to the girl's cottage," she said, turning and pointing through the big arched window that overlooked the landing. I saw, across the parking lot, the house the caseworker had showed us when we arrived, the yellow one with brown trim and a second-story bay window.

The nursery was in the second-floor veranda. As we walked towards the veranda's large double doors, Mrs. Knutson explained about the staff not allowing older boys in the nursery and making an exception for me because of it being my second day and about not having time to make friends. She threw in some other things, but her words got lost because by that time I was doing all I could just to keep up with her.

The nursery was a large, bright, airy space with continuous columns of windows on three sides extending almost up to the ceiling. Below the windows, a long plain wooden chest ran the full length of the room. It contained an assortment of toys, most of which were aged or broken. I saw a doll with its head missing and another one with its arm dangling by a thread.

A jungle gym took up half the floor space on the right side of the room and it reached almost to the ceiling. I had played on a jungle gym when we lived in Morgan Park, but I had never seen one inside a house before. One little boy was holding on to the lowest metal handrail and swinging back and forth; I had a hard time imaging him trying to climb to the top.

The nursery was a bedlam of noise and activity. Some of the children were still in diapers, and almost all of them were crawling or wobbling about, jabbering, falling, and bumping into whoever or whatever got in their way. A beautiful young woman with dimples and a big smile on her face walked up, and Mrs. Knutson introduced her to me. "This is Miss Kelly. She is the supervisor of the second floor and she's in charge of the nursery.

Miss Kelly was my first love and I vowed on the spot that I would marry her one day. She had long, light brown, wavy hair and she wore a pleated cotton dress with a wide matching belt that showed off a narrow waist. Her face was flawless and as smooth as silk. She had a delicate nose, big blue eyes, and tantalizing lips, but most of all she had a bubbly personality. I could tell right away that she loved children.

"Hi, who's this good looking young man?" she asked as she bent over and took my hand.

"This is Terry. He's the *big* brother of Jean and Larry Haataja," said Mrs. Knutson.

"Welcome to the nursery, Terry. Would you like to go and say hi to your sister and brother while I talk to Mrs. Knutson?"

Mrs. Knutson cut in. "I'm sorry. I hope you don't mind. I told Terry you might make an exception and let him stay in the nursery for a few days, until he gets to know some of the older children. Would you mind?"

"I guess we could make an exception," Miss Kelly said, looking down at me with a smile, "but by the weekend, I'll bet you'll be outside with the older boys."

Not wanting to disagree, not with her anyway, I nodded and started looking for my sister and brother. Within seconds, I spotted Jean cradling a doll and standing by several girls her age behind the jungle gym. I walked over to her and asked, "Where is Larry?"

"He's over there," Jean said, pointing to a small group of boys playing on the other side of the room.

"Where?"

"He's wearing a red-and-white striped shirt. They gave us new clothes because Mom forgot to bring ours."

I spotted the striped shirt, but it wasn't until Larry yanked a toy out of a boy's hands and yelled, "It's mine!" that I recognized him. Unlike me, Larry was big for his age. When he wanted something, he just took it.

CHAPTER 17
The Great Escape

The two weeks following our induction into the Children's Home were excruciatingly painful for me, and it must have been heartbreaking for staff members to watch. Every day, without fail, I would ask Miss Kelly, or any other matron who happened to cross paths with me, when my mom was coming. I continued to wet the bed, and I refused to stay anywhere but the nursery, where I brooded and generally made a nuisance of myself. Despite this, Miss Kelly let me stay in the nursery, but she made it perfectly clear from the start that it was a temporary situation. According to her, I should be outside playing with the older boys, which was somewhat paradoxical to me, since I was both the smallest boy on the third floor and the youngest.

[According to an old newspaper article, the Children's Home did not accept babies under the age of six months, and I don't recall seeing any babies in the nursery who weren't at least crawling. Jean, who was three at the time, was one of the "older" girls, and Larry, at two, was probably the median age. So I was, no question about it, the oldest child in the nursery.]

There were twelve or fifteen of us in the nursery at that time—enough to keep Miss Kelly busy. It was obvious from the beginning that I didn't fit in. For starters, most of the children were not big enough to pull themselves up to the first rung of the jungle gym, let alone the top. I did it because I could, and to show off. Some of the children, especially my brother Larry, tried to follow. This kept Miss Kelly busy either helping them or pulling them off when it looked like they were ready to fall. Eventually, she told me to stay off the gym, which made her job easier, but it took away the only physical activity I had going for me.

I have always been a physically active person, so without the jungle gym to keep me occupied, I started to get antsy. I pestered Miss Kelly constantly about what I could do, until, in frustration, she brought in a Tinker Toy set. Because of its smaller pieces, she made me take it to one corner of the room, away from the other children. For a few days, at least, building things like windmills and castles kept my mind engaged. However, when a key piece went missing, which it often did, or when one of the toddlers tripped over a half-finished project, sending parts flying all over the place, I would call for Miss Kelly, and she would try her best to calm me down. After one such incident, she helped me put a half-completed house back together, and when I complained about a missing piece, she said, "I'm afraid you'll have to do without it because the piece was probably missing when the box was donated to the Home."

Jean made friends easily, and she adapted quickly to her new surroundings. She spent most of her time playing house with the other girls. I can see her now walking around with a doll in her arms, her blonde hair catching rays of light filtering in from the windows, pretending to be the doll's mother and chatting with it and scolding it as if it were a real child.

I can't say with any certainty that Larry adapted to his new environment or that he got along with children his own age, because I stayed away from him as much as I could. It didn't take long for Miss Kelly to learn that it was in her own best interests to keep us apart. It seemed like whenever we were together, things got out of hand. Larry would, without apparent provocation, walk over to where I was sitting and kick or brush aside whatever it was I was working on. I suppose this was a form of sibling rivalry, but it tended to be one sided. I would get upset, complain, and Miss Kelly would separate us again.

The first weekend came, and for two days, I nagged the staff about our mother's whereabouts. I ran to the first story veranda whenever a car drove by. In the nursery, I stood by the window for hours, my forehead pressed against the glass in hopes of seeing her. When she didn't show, my irritation increased, and I became even more withdrawn and sullen.

From the beginning, I pestered Jean about running away. At first, she was reluctant, but she soon became both a willing listener and a co-conspirator. I had a picture in my mind of seeing the Aerial Lift Bridge from Aunt Irene's. I reasoned that all we had to do to make our escape was walk down to the bridge. I mean, after all, if we could see the bridge from Irene's house, surely we would be able to see her house from the bridge. We had to get away from the Children's Home and from the Witch, Mrs. Scheidler, who, Jean and I agreed, was responsible for taking us away from our mother.

[It is impossible to say how many days passed before we made our great escape because there is no record of the day our

mother put us into the Children's Home. Here is what I do
know. I know that we were still at Aunt Irene's on April 1, and
I think I can safely assume that some time passed before our
mother made the necessary arrangements for our incarceration.
I also have a record of the date of our escape. It was Friday,
April 21, 1950.]

Shortly after breakfast, I walked over to Jean and whispered,
"Let's go."

She looked at me with her big blue eyes and said, "OK, but
I hope we don't get caught, because we'll get into trouble."

"We won't. We'll find Mom and she'll fix everything. You'll
see."

We went over to where Larry was playing and Jean told him
we were leaving. When he asked where we were going, she said,
"We're going to see Mom." Without a word, Larry laid down
his toy and followed us out of the nursery. Holding hands, we
walked down the stairs and out the side door to freedom.

CHAPTER 18
Riding High

It was warm for that time of the year. The sun was high enough to take the chill out of the air, and there wasn't a cloud in sight. From where we stood on the Children's Home steps, we could clearly see the harbor, which had lost much of its winter coat of ice. The trees were still naked and the lawns were an ugly brown, but almost all of the winter snow had melted.

Larry and I wore long-sleeved flannel shirts and corduroy pants held up with suspenders. Jean wore a long-sleeved dress with pants and her favorite dark brown winter boots. She wore them everywhere. I remember her picking them out at the store. They zipped up in the front and there was fur around the top. She had begged Mom to buy them for her because they looked just like Mom's boots. We were used to cold weather, so bringing our winter coats never entered our minds. Besides, I didn't know where mine was or if our mother had even bothered to bring it.

Holding hands, we walked down the steps to the sidewalk,

and from there we headed downtown. It's easy to find the retail district in Duluth, even for someone our age. The city, built on the side of a cliff, overlooks Lake Superior and the Duluth harbor, and the most visible sight in the harbor is the Aerial Lift Bridge. I was confident that all we had to do was to go down by the bridge, and when we got there, we would see Aunt Irene's house.

The going was easy at first—we were excited about going home, we were nourished, and we were walking downhill. Jean insisted on holding hands whenever we crossed a street. I think it was more for Larry's sake. He was still young and he tended to hang back when left unattended. By the time we reached the middle of the third crosswalk, Larry started grumbling about going back. "My feet hurt," he kept saying. From that point on, I had to retrace my steps at almost every intersection, grab his arm, and drag him, which wasn't an easy thing to do because, at two, Larry was almost as big as Jean. By the time we had gone ten blocks and after passing several people, many of whom were old men loitering on the side of buildings or at the entrance to alleys, I had begun to have grave doubts about my grand scheme. It dawned on me that asking complete strangers for directions wasn't going to work. I didn't have Mom's address, and even if the person we asked knew our mother, how would they know where she lived? In other words, the world suddenly got a lot bigger and I got a lot smaller.

I kept these negative thoughts to myself until Jean said, "Aren't you going to ask?"

By this time, we were in the middle of downtown, where people were scurrying about going from one store to another, and cars and buses were jamming the streets. Once a woman stopped us and asked where we were going, and when I answered, "We're going home," she just shrugged and kept walking. Other than the woman, no one talked to us, which was fine with me.

"*You* ask," I said.

"You promised you were going to ask someone when we got downtown!" she cried, tears starting to roll down her cheeks. "I'm not big enough, and you promised."

Seeing her tears, I moved close to her and said, "I don't think they know our mom, and they don't know where Aunt Irene lives." By this time, I was convinced that my plan was hopeless—we were in the wrong section of the city. The buildings were taller and cars and buses were everywhere. In the part of town where Aunt Irene lived, the buildings were smaller and the traffic not nearly as busy. In addition, from Irene's I could see the big iron ore loading docks from her front window. From where we stood, the loading docks were nowhere in sight.

"If we can't find Mom, where are we going to go?" Jean asked, frightened. I didn't have a ready answer for her. I stood at her side looking lost and confused. After a while, she said, "Maybe we can find a policeman—he'll know."

At once, Larry started jumping up and down, shouting, "Let's find a policeman, I want to find a policeman!"

I thought about this for a few seconds, and then I said, "OK, a policeman would know where Aunt Irene lives. Maybe he even knows our mom." This satisfied Jean. She wiped her tears and smiled. With a new purpose and renewed energy, we started looking for a police officer. Soon, I thought, we would be home and everything would be the way it had been before Mrs. Scheidler took us away from our mother.

After several more blocks of walking, we found ourselves at the waterfront and on a sidewalk leading to the Aerial Lift

Bridge. We had two choices. We could either turn around and walk back up the hill to continue our search for a policeman, or we could keep going to the lift bridge in the hope that we would find one there. I did not want to consider the alternative.

"What about those houses on the other side of the bridge?" Jean asked. "Maybe that's where Aunt Irene lives!" Off in the distance, I saw buildings and another downtown district. The buildings were smaller, and it didn't look as busy as the downtown district we had just passed. A long, narrow strip of land that looked like a beach with water on both sides separated the bridge from the town. Buildings dotted the sandy landscape, which, except for the traffic, was completely devoid of people.

"If we go to the bridge, maybe we can see the house from there," I said, desperately wanting to believe it. I shivered as the cold winds sweeping off Lake Superior penetrated my shirt. Exhausted and feeling pangs of hunger and cold, I wanted this to end. I wanted to go home and I wanted my mom.

Holding each other's hands, we walked toward the bridge. We passed some industrial buildings along the way and a few cars sped by, but we didn't see a policeman or even a pedestrian. Maybe the people were all at work, or maybe the frigid air was keeping them away from the waterfront. Whatever the reason, we were completely alone—cut off from everything and everyone, in the center of a busy seaport, just a few blocks from downtown Duluth. Somehow, it didn't seem real.

We reached the bridge, and seeing no one, walked across, hearing the rattle of cars and an occasional horn from an unhappy driver. Looking out across Lake Superior, I saw a lane of open water between floating ice sheets. The ice was beginning to break up, depositing large chunks in piles on the beach. In the distance, I saw a large freighter heading in our direction.

"What is that thing over there?" Jean suddenly asked.

I turned and looked to see her pointing at something. It was an iron gate. Behind it a staircase wound its way up to a landing high above us and on the landing stood a little white house. I stared at the house for a few seconds and then an idea hit me. "Maybe we can see Aunt Irene's house from up there," I said.

Jean shook her head, "No, we can't, because we'll get into trouble! Anyway, the gate is locked!"

"I want to climb way up!" screeched Larry. Before I could stop him, he ran over to the gate and, like a rabbit, he slithered under it. Running to stop him, I reached over the railing and grabbed his arm, but he wiggled free. With his fat, stubby legs, he began to climb. Jean and I went under the gate too, and soon we were all standing on the landing high above the water. The bridge vibrated and I heard and felt the tires of cars as they hit the many potholes in the bridge's road. Off in the distance, I saw the freighter nearing the harbor entrance, and to our right I saw the rooftops of the buildings in the downtown shopping district.

"Can you see Aunt Irene's house?" asked Jean. Squinting, I searched among the buildings beyond the sandy strip of land, but nothing looked familiar. It had to be out there, but where? All of a sudden, the blast of a loud horn filled the air, followed by loud metallic squealing, and then the platform beneath us began to jerk.

"Lay down!" I screamed, my heart racing. "I think the bridge is going up!" We dropped and lay flat against the platform's steel grate.

"What are we going to do?" cried Jean, confused and afraid. "We can't stay here, we'll fall!"

"No, we won't," I said, "not if we stay still and don't move."

Larry yelped, "Whee, this fun! We going in the sky!" The road below and the platform we were standing on began to rise in unison, and not at an angle, like some other bridges I had seen, but straight up, like an elevator. Except this elevator wasn't enclosed, and we weren't inside. The platform kept going higher and higher. Then, just when it seemed like we were going to touch the clouds, the bridge, with loud screeching and banging, came to a sudden stop. When the vibrations settled, I looked down through the square holes at the cars and people lined up by the side of the bridge.

"Look," I said, the people look like little ants."

"Yeah, they look like ants," echoed Larry.

Turning my head, I noticed that the bow of the freighter I had seen earlier was now even with the lighthouses at the ends of the two long piers jutting out into Lake Superior on both sides of the bridge. "Look!" I shouted, "The freighter's going to go under the bridge!" This was exciting!

Suddenly, we were startled by a loud male voice. "What are you kids doing here?" It was an older man in coveralls, his hands on his hips and a severe look on his face. "How did you kids get up here? Then he darted into his little house but soon returned, saying, "The police are on the way. If I had room in the control house, I'd have you come in here, but it's too small. I want you to stay put. Will you do that for me?" he asked in a stern voice while shaking his finger at us.

We all nodded yes. He stared at us. I guess he wanted to make sure we weren't going to run away, which didn't make sense to me. Where could we go? If we ran back down the stairs, we'd have to climb over the gate and jump to the street, which was a long way down, and also we might land in the water instead. So, since we did not intend to go anywhere, we all turned our attention back to the ship as it moved past the lighthouses at the ends of the piers, watching in excited fascination as it glided beneath us, its mast almost touching the bridge. Men moved on its spotless reddish-brown deck. Some were standing against the railings, while others attended to their duties. I felt as though I could have reached out and pushed it along like a toy boat.

After the ship had sailed into the harbor, I became aware of the sirens and flashing lights of police cars as they pulled up to the side of the bridge. Men and women were getting out of their cars and waving at us. I waved back. Thank goodness, I thought. We found our police officer. Now we can go home.

CHAPTER 19

A Severe Behavior Problem

This was a rather severe behavior problem. Child was brought into the hospital at 11:50 am on Friday, the 21st of April 1950 largely to keep under observation and see what could be done about training. This is a broken home and the mother-child relationship is not good. During the hospital stay the child was taught to obey and responded well and was a fairly well behaved child at the time of his discharge on the 28th of April, 1950 – **St. Mary's Hospital Records**

The police escorted us from the bridge towards their waiting cars. We were tired, hungry, and chilled by the Lake Superior wind, but instead of putting us into a warm squad car, the police split us up for questioning. I guess they thought we would spill our guts quicker if we were separated and in a state of frozen anxiety. The officer who took me aside was grim and serious. He asked what we were doing on the bridge, and I told him we were looking for our mom. When he asked where we lived, I told him I didn't know the address. With my teeth chattering uncontrollably, I tried my best to describe where the house was in relationship to the Aerial Lift Bridge. I explained about being able to see the bridge and the iron ore ships from the front window and about the nearby loading docks, and I may have even told him it was Aunt Irene's and not our mom's house. At no time, however, did I say anything about the orphanage. It was probably Larry who did the tattling, because I heard the police officer standing next to him shout "They're from the Children's Home!" I knew instantly that they would take us back to the orphanage, and so, instead of continuing to plead with the officer to bring us to our mother, I took off running down the beach toward the lake. I didn't have a plan, but I was not going back to the orphanage, so I ran into the freezing cold water, screaming, "You can't make me go back! I want to see my mom!"

The next thing I remember is sitting in the back seat of a squad car as it pulled up in front of the Children's Home. I was by myself—naked and wrapped in a blanket. My body was shaking violently, my teeth still chattering, as the officer lifted me out and carried me up the steps.

The reunion with the staff was not a happy one. Despite my nakedness and the exhaustion I felt from the morning's activities and the cold water shock treatment, I continued to be full of fight. I kept screaming, "I want to see my mom!" I refused to eat, and I spat at the matrons who, with a certain amount of physical force, managed to clothe me. To them, it must have looked like I was completely out of control, but I was actually well aware of my behavior: I was intentionally acting out. I thought that my actions would force them to call my mother, but instead, someone, probably the Witch, made the decision to take me to the hospital.

Strangely, considering everything else I remember, I do not

have a memory of the ride to the hospital, only bits and pieces of our arrival. Someone from the orphanage carried me inside. When he tried to stand me on my feet, I went limp and slid to the floor. It was my way of breaking free from his grasp, and it worked for a moment, but he quickly grabbed my arm again. This time, instead of carrying me, he dragged me down a short hallway and into a lobby or waiting room, with me screaming at the top of my lungs. The scene must have been upsetting for the patients or visitors who happened to be in the lobby that day, but I took no notice of them or of the surroundings.

I was still limp when I felt the man's grip slacken. I jerked hard enough to free my arm, but I was not able to support myself, and I landed on the floor with a thud. The man grabbed me from behind and wrestled me onto my stomach, his knee in the small of my back, my cheeks pushed flat against the cold black-and-white checkered tile. As I lay there struggling to breathe, I heard footsteps. Tilting my head, I saw a pair of white nylons and the torso of a woman in a white dress. The woman carried what looked like a striped gray-and-white jacket with long strings dangling from the sleeves. I heard her say, "Here, put this on. It'll restrain him until I can give him something to calm him down."

The strong arms of the man pulled me up off the floor. He held my arms behind my back while I continued to kick and scream, trying my best to break free. Then he forced my arms into the sleeves of the jacket. "Here, grab the straps and tie them behind his back," he said. I kicked backward, hitting him in the shin. "Ouch! Jesus, you little *shit*!" the man exclaimed, reaching down to rub his leg.

"Let me go! I'll kill you! I'll kill you! I'll get a gun and shoot you!" I screamed hysterically. I squirmed and tugged as hard as

I could, and then I heard a snap followed by a ripping sound as my right arm broke free. I started to run, frantically trying to pull the rest of the restraint off, but I didn't get far before I again felt the man's hands on me. This time he put an arm around my waist and lifted me up in the air.

"He broke the string, get another one!" he yelled, squeezing me tight against his body.

A few minutes later, the woman came back with another restraint, but again I broke the string. They were successful on the third attempt. Perhaps this time the restraint was stronger—I recall hearing someone say, "He won't get out of this one." More likely, I was just exhausted.

The man carried me into a large room filled with cribs. Not baby cribs, but extra large cribs, built for older children. He hoisted me into the one nearest the door and forced me to lie down. I stayed in that position, continuing half-heartedly to try to free myself. When the man finally stepped away, I worked myself toward the head of the crib. Using the headboard for leverage, I scrambled to my feet. Spent, but still in a heightened state of anxiety, I looked wildly around the room. Two adults were staring at me. In an identical crib stood another young boy. "Stop staring at me!" I yelled. This must have startled the poor boy, because he started crying. I looked over at the adults and repeated my previous threat: "I'm going to get a gun and kill you! I'll kill you!" Then, someone grabbed me and held me, and I felt the prick of a needle in my arm. That's the last thing I remember about my stay at the hospital.

A metamorphosis of sorts took place that day. It was, I believe, at that moment that I changed from a happy, inquisitive little boy into an angry man-child. I experienced, for the first time, a total loss of control of my little world. It changed my outlook on life and weakened my trust in mankind.

[Studies have shown that orphans who are not adopted soon after birth are highly intuitive. They have a heightened sense of danger, a mistrust of authority, and a low sense of self-worth. My life is a testament to the aforementioned disorders. Other signs include anger and pushing oneself to a state of total exhaustion, behavior also displayed that day at the hospital. It's a stressful psychosis, and for me it would lead to some interesting, if not dangerous, experiences later in life.]

CHAPTER 20
A Legend

With the exception of my grand entrance, I have no memory of the seven days I spent at St. Mary's Hospital. According to a reliable source, the doctor prescribed Phenobarbital to calm me down. I will never know if I received any treatment or comforting beyond that because many of the records from that time were lost in a fire. I don't recall seeing my mother at the hospital, but considering the diagnosis, it's quite possible the doctor in charge of the case had decided against bringing us together. Someone had apprised her of what happened, however, because I clearly remember her asking me if I had really told a man that I would get a gun and shoot him.

The staff at the orphanage treated me like a returning hero. Evidently my exploits were already legendary. "Did you really threaten to shoot somebody?" "Did you really climb to the top of the Aerial Lift Bridge?" asked the matrons. Years later, two other sources backed up this account of my return. The legend lives on!

But life slowed for me after my release from the hospital. The Phenobarbital doses continued twice a day through the summer and into the fall. The drug kept me out of trouble, but it also left me in a perpetual state of tranquil disorientation. At breakfast time the pill would be in a pleated white paper cup next to my plate, and at bedtime the nurse would say, "Here's your pill. Remember, take just a small sip of the water. We don't want to wet the bed, do we?"

I was in this state when I started to become acclimated to life at the orphanage. Like the other boys, I learned to make my own bed and to pick up after myself, and like them, I was responsible for putting my dirty clothes and linens into the laundry chute. When I returned in the evening, my clean clothes and linens would be folded and lying on my bed. I also learned that there were consequences for not following rules. I made the mistake once of getting to dinner late and ended up in the kitchen washing pots and pans.

I was assigned to the Naughty Room just a day or two after my release. Mrs. Dettborn walked me to the dorm and told me to pick up my things and follow her. I had no idea where she was taking me. All she said was, "You're lucky. You're going to get your very own room." She ushered me down the hall to a large heavy door next to the steps. Unlike the swinging double doors that led into the boy's dorm, this door was like any other door its size, with one exception. Above the door was a rectangular window. The glass wasn't flat with the wall but slanted horizontally for the purpose, I assumed, of admitting air into the room or into the hallway or a little of both. Mrs. Dettborn opened the door and ushered me in. The room was spacious and rectangular in shape, with a dormer window that overlooked Chester Park. It had a dresser, two bunk beds, and a small washroom with a toilet and sink.

"How come I have to be here?" I asked.

"Well, we thought you would like to have your own room so the other boys won't tease you about wetting the bed."

I don't recall getting teased, but I do remember the shame I felt, and of course she was right; if I had stayed in the boys' dorm any longer, I'm sure the teasing would have followed. I also have to believe the move had something to do with my running away and my classification as a "severe disciplinary case."

She asked which bed I wanted. Happy to have my pick, I chose the one across from the door to the bathroom. She pulled a rubber pad from one of the dresser drawers and put it on top of the mattress.

"From now on, I want you to use this pad, and before you go to breakfast, I want you to wash your sheets in the bathroom sink and then throw them down the chute."

"Won't they see me?"

"If you do it right, no one will even notice, and you don't have to wash the whole sheet, just the stain."

She showed me what she meant, and then I asked, "What if I don't wet the bed?"

"Well, that would be good. Then you don't have to wash your sheets. Do you think you could stop?"

"Uh-huh! I'm not going to do it anymore!" I said proudly. Unfortunately, I didn't live up to my word.

Now that I had my own room I was pretty much free to come and go as I wished, at least for a time. So I moped around the room instead of the nursery, which had been declared off limits to me. Only Larry remained there, because Miss Kelly encouraged Jean to play outside with girls closer to her age.

Then one day, a male staffer came into my room and asked, "Terry, did you know your sister is eating green army worms?"

"No," I said, screwing up my face. I couldn't imagine her eating any worms, let alone green ones. "Did she really?"

"Yup! I saw her pick up a worm from the top of the fence and put it in her mouth." He paused, looked down at me, and said, "Don't you think it would be a good idea if you kept an eye on your sister?"

I looked at him for a few seconds, trying to figure out if he was telling the truth, but failing this, I asked, "Where is she?"

"She's out back in the fenced-in area. Do you want me to show you?" he asked, holding out his hand. I didn't take it, but I did follow him.

The fenced-in playground was on the back side of the Children's Home between the alley and the neighbor's yard. The fence kept the children from wandering off, and it kept the need for supervision to a minimum. Round wooden posts, painted forest green and planted twelve feet apart, served as a frame for the metal mesh fence. Nailed to the top of the posts were green two-by-six boards. The yard had a swing set, teeter-totters, and a large sandbox, but there was still plenty of room for the children to run around.

"Where did the worm come from?" I asked, as he stepped aside to let me pass through the one and only gate.

"Right over there on top of the fence," he replied, pointing in the general direction of the neighbor's house.

I knew Jean wasn't tall enough to reach the top of the fence, and I wondered how anyone could see a green worm on a board painted the same color.

When I asked Jean about it later, she wrinkled up her face and said, "Yuk, I didn't eat a worm! That's dumb!" If I asked her the same question today, she would say the same thing, in the same manner, and with the same emphasis. I've always suspected the worm story was just a ploy to get me outside, and it worked, because from then on I kept a close watch over my sister.

I came down with measles in 1950, around the time I started kindergarten. This must have been an inconvenience for the staff, because they had just gotten rid of me by sending me outdoors. Now here I was back in my room and an even bigger nuisance, because now they had to wait on me hand and foot. The thing I remember the most about being bedridden was the food: watery soup and dry, tasteless sandwiches. Years later, a staff member from that time told me the bland food was intentional—it was a disincentive to get the children out of bed and outdoors as quickly as possible. I was also vaccinated for smallpox and diphtheria around that time, and I was given the Wasserman test, which came back negative. [The test is for syphilis, but in those days, they also used it to screen for tuberculosis—an application later proven to be unreliable.]

In July of 1950 Jean, Larry, and I took a Greyhound to Grandma and Grandpa's farm. Our mother, for unknown reasons, did not accompany us on the trip. I remember the fuss a woman at the station made over us as we were getting on the bus, and how indifferent the driver acted during the trip as Larry ran up and down the aisle pestering the other passengers.

When the bus stopped for fuel, Larry got off and had lunch in a roadside diner with the couple who had been sitting four seats behind us; Jean and I remained in the bus. When I confronted him later about getting off the bus with strangers, he said, "They told me I could eat with them."

"Did they know we were on the bus too?" I asked, knowing

the answer. I had seen the man eyeing us during the first leg of the trip.

"I told them, and they said they didn't have enough money for you and they liked me the best anyway," Larry said with a smug look.

The man and woman were one of the youngest couples on the bus. The man had curly, black hair and rugged features, and the pupils of his eyes were unusual. They were large, almost black, and matched his black eyebrows. Once, when I turned around to see what Larry was doing, the man looked directly into my eyes, and I got this creepy feeling that he was looking right through me. His wife had long brown hair, dainty features, and a gentle, soothing voice that was difficult to hear.

For some reason the couple stopped talking to Larry after the bus resumed its journey. He had walked back to their seat, but I heard the man tell him to go back and sit down. I think this irritated Larry, because he came back to us in a huff. When the couple got off the bus in Virginia, Minnesota they walked by us without saying a word.

The days and nights at Grandma and Grandpa's were boring compared to the excitement of the Children's Home. Just as before, we played outside by ourselves. We also went to the lake once, but not much else happened.

The yard was littered with more junk than usual, including a Model A resting on its axle by the woodshed. The Model A that Grandpa drove sat next to the fishing shack. Piles of wood were everywhere, and a large flatbed trailer loaded with white birch rested next to the garage. In the dirt by the house lay a rusting old car hood, and metal containers of all sizes and shapes were scattered helter-skelter.

Time on the farm moved swiftly. Before I realized it, we

were back on the bus to the orphanage. This time the trip went without incident. I was asleep before the bus got to Virginia and I didn't wake up until we pulled into Duluth. As far as I know, Larry behaved. And I was happy to be going back to the comforts of the Children's Home.

CHAPTER 21
Confused

I turned five that summer, and in the fall, I entered kinder-garten. For years I told people, including my own children, that I went to the "Indian School." I would later learn it was really the *Endion* School. One of the matrons accompanied me for orientation day, but from that point on, I walked with other orphans or, as was most often the case, by myself. That was because I had to stay late to wash my sheets. I will never forget that six-block walk. If pressed, I could probably describe some of the cracks in the sidewalk, and I most certainly could draw a map of every alley and shortcut. It was common for me to arrive in the classroom just as the bell rang, but sometimes I arrived so late that I found the door to the classroom locked. To get in, I had to go to the principal's office, and after a short lecture, someone from the office would escort me to the class-room.

My memory of the teacher and of the other kids in the class-room is sketchy at best, probably because of the Phenobarbital.

I do remember lying on a reed mat and a classmate encouraging me to look up the teacher's dress when she walked over my head. I wondered why the teacher walked over the children's heads and not around them, but I also remember telling the boy it was stupid to look up the teacher's dress. I have also had flashbacks about a boy who brought a sword to class for show-and-tell. I walked with the boy after school and I asked him if I could see the blade. He pulled it part way out of its sheath, and I studied it closely. It had an ornate handle and an elaborate etched design. I thought the boy might have been stretching the truth or maybe even lying about his great grandpa using it in the Civil War, because I didn't see a nick or a scratch on the blade.

The only thing I remember about classroom activities is the frustration I felt when I tried to stay within the lines while coloring. Whenever I slipped with my crayon, an art I seem to have mastered, my irritation would quickly surface, and I would scribble all over the page. The teacher would walk over to my desk and say, "That's OK, Terry," in a soft, soothing voice—a voice that drove me crazy. "You'll get better. You just need to work at it more." I didn't get better. I struggled with coloring for the rest of that year, or at least until I stopped taking Phenobarbital.

I don't think there's any question the drug contributed to my inability to focus. Besides having the coloring problem, it wasn't uncommon for me to sit at my desk and stare out the window for hours at a time. Sometimes the teacher would direct a question at me, and when I wouldn't respond, she would shout my name or walk over to my desk and tap on it until I came out of my trance. Once I just wandered off by myself. I think it happened after recess, and I don't think I actually went anywhere—I just stayed outside after the bell rang. Anyway, someone spotted me and escorted me back to the classroom. He said something like, "I saw him wandering off" and that became the official verdict.

Eventually the effects of the drug on my behavior concerned the teacher to the point where she must have felt obligated to take action. She wrote a letter and asked me to carry it home with instructions to give it to the superintendent at the orphanage. The teacher didn't tell me what was in the letter, but not long after I gave it to Mrs. Scheidler, I was taken off the medication.

I'd like to say this change had a positive impact on my education, but I'd be lying. I awoke to find that I was behind the rest of my classmates. As learning deficits go, it was minuscule, but it was enough to affect my attitude. Instead of making an effort to catch up, I withdrew into a shell, falling even further behind, and the orphanage, as will be seen, did not provide a positive environment for education.

CHAPTER 22
The Shortcut

A blizzard dumped over twenty-five inches of snow on Duluth between the fifth and eighth of December that year. Schools closed for the week, but by the beginning of the following week, the blizzard had subsided and the schools reopened.

Monday turned out to be a beautiful day—the sky was bright blue and cloudless without a trace of wind. However, it was still freezing cold outside, and it wasn't much better indoors. After washing my sheets, I gathered my winter duds, which I got from the Salvation Army, and I walked down to the east door to get help with putting them on. My rubber boots, which were a size too large, had a thick inner lining that always came out when I pulled them off. The tops were made of canvas and a pull string kept the snow from getting inside. I had a black aviator's hat with a strap that snapped under my chin, a bulky winter jacket that made it difficult for me to move, and baggy snow pants. The pants had a hole in the right knee, showing the white insulating material beneath, and the suspenders had to be bunched up and pinned to keep the pants from falling down.

"I can't get it in," I said, shoving the safety pin toward Miss Kelly, who had just finished helping another boy with his mittens. As always, I was the last one in line and the last to leave for school. She pulled up my suspenders until they were tight, overlapped the excess material, stuck the pin through, and locked it in place. "There," she said, "that should do it. Let's get your coat and mittens on and you can get on your way."

I ran down the steps to the sidewalk and hurried toward school. It didn't dawn on me that I had forgotten to pick up my lunch bag until the end of the first block, but by then it was too late. By the second block, I knew I had to make a decision to either keep going and deal with the consequences of getting to school late, or take the shortcut that went through an empty lot. The matrons had warned us not to take this route, but it was either that or the principal's office, so I chose the shortcut.

When I arrived at the lot, I looked across and saw nothing but windswept snowdrifts. With everything white, it was impossible to tell how deep the snow was. The crossing started out fine. The snow came up to the top of my boots and I made good time, but as I worked my way toward the center, the snow got deeper and deeper. By the time I was a third of the way across, it was up to my waist and getting higher by the second. Because of the high winds that had accompanied the blizzard, the snow was heavier than normal, and it had formed a thin top crust that broke through as the weight of my body plowed into it.

By the time I reached the middle of the lot, the snow was up to my chest, I was exhausted, and for the first time, scared. Tears rolled down my cheeks. Each step was excruciatingly difficult—it felt like I was climbing a steep hill. I would lift my foot as high as I could and push forward with all my weight. Then I would pause, lift the other foot, and push forward again. This went on for an eternity. The only thing preventing me from falling on my face was the firmness of the snow. Once, I even tried to crawl on the crust, but it wasn't firm enough to hold me. I ended up getting snow all over my face, which only added to my fright and discomfort. I had a difficult time seeing where I was going, and the end was nowhere in sight. I looked back several times and seriously considered backtracking, but all I could think of was how mad the principal was going to be. This thought kept me plugging forward. Finally, about three-quarters of the way across, the depth of the snow decreased until it was boot deep again. I heaved a sigh of relief and started running, hoping that I could still make it to school before the bell rang.

As it turned out, I was over thirty minutes late. When I told the principal and the teacher what happened, they reprimanded me. And someone must have called the orphanage, because when I returned, I got a tongue-lashing and was sent straight to bed without the evening meal—a common disciplinary procedure at the Children's Home.

CHAPTER 23

To Grandma's House We Go

A few weeks after the blizzard, Mrs. Scheidler informed me that we were going to our grandparents' house for Christmas. On the morning of our departure, I awoke in the fetal position. My nose, the only part of my body sticking out from under the blanket, felt as if someone had placed it in the freezer overnight. Pulling the covers over my head, I listened to the wind as it whipped against the dorm window and the rhythmic sound of metal banging against metal.

Gathering my courage, I threw the blankets off, and immediately regretted the decision. The room, as usual, was uncomfortably cold, and it didn't improve when my feet hit the frozen hardwood floor. With my teeth chattering and my arms crossed over my chest, I scampered into the bathroom. I used the toilet, brushed my teeth, and returned to the bedroom, where I hurriedly threw on some clothes. Afterwards, I made the bed, ran downstairs, and ate a quick breakfast. I spent the rest of the morning wandering aimlessly from one room to another, annoying the staff by repeatedly asking for the time. Around ten o'clock, Jean, Larry, and I put on our winter clothes and, with permission from Mrs. Scheidler, went to the veranda to wait. Huddling together for warmth, we listened to the unrelenting wind as it swirled through the grated gates at the foundation, finding its way up through the cracks in the floorboards. Ice covered the windows, in some spots as thick as an inch. Our breath hung in the air, but we were too excited to care.

"Maybe we should make a hole in the window. That way we can see them when they come," Jean said, breaking the silence.

I walked over to the window next to the front door and put my face close to the glass. I blew a stream of warm air against it, creating a small circle of melted ice. Then I rubbed hard with my mitten. A small opening appeared through which I could see the street, but it frosted over within seconds. After several more attempts, I gave up in frustration, choosing instead to open the door whenever I heard the sound of a car. This annoyed Mrs. Scheidler, and she came out to the veranda in a huff. "Terry, is that you opening the door all the time? I feel a draft in my office every time you do it. I want you to stop."

Mrs. Scheidler's office window, which overlooked the veranda and almost filled the entire right side of the brick wall, reminded me of the stained glass windows at church. It didn't have a colorful picture of a saint or Jesus, but it did have a large arched center pane encased within a thick wood frame. Surrounding that pane were six smaller ones.

"Why don't you kids come inside where it's warm?" she asked. "I'm sure your mom will come in when she gets here." We just stared at her. After a few seconds of silence, she threw up her arms in frustration and went back inside.

I'm not sure how long we waited. I know that Mrs. Scheidler

came back several times, and I know that we all went to the bathroom at least once. Larry finally got antsy. He went inside to play with some friends until I got mad and yelled, "They're coming, Larry. You better get out here!" They weren't, of course, but I knew my brother. Given enough time, he would get lost, and we'd spend a half-hour searching for him.

Shortly before noon, I heard a car come to a stop in front of the Home. Opening the door a crack, I saw Mom sitting in the passenger seat of Uncle Alan's old jalopy. She opened the car door, but before her feet had time to touch the ground, we were at her side. We jumped into the back seat, excited to be on our way. Meanwhile, Uncle Alan had taken a blanket from the car trunk. "Here," he said, throwing it at us, "the heater's not working. Huddle together and put the blanket around you."

"You mean there's no heat in the back seat?" our mother asked, tucking the blanket around us. "Alan, we have a two hour drive!"

"I know," he replied, "but what can I do? There's some heat, but it's not much. Here, take this scraper. I need you to keep my window clear."

Uncle Alan's car was a 1934 Ford Victoria Coupe. In addition to having dented fenders, a faded paint job, and an interior that smelled like mildew, the car relied on an antiquated air re-circulating system. In weather conditions above forty degrees, the heater worked fine, but when the temperature dropped below zero, as it had on this particular day, the system was almost useless.

With no heat, frost on the windows, and a strong wind whipping snow across the highway, Alan drove at a snail's pace. From the back seat, I watched as Mom kept scraping the front window while Uncle Alan, leaning forward in his seat, used the heat from his hand to make a small opening that disappeared almost as quickly as it appeared. Meanwhile the three of us huddled together on the edge of our seat to get as much heat from the front as we could. As it had on the veranda, the wind whistled through cracks in the car, making it almost impossible for us to carry on a conversation. What would normally have taken less than two hours took up most of the afternoon, but finally I heard Uncle Alan shout, "We're here!"

Excited, I sat up and stretched my neck to see out of the small opening in Alan's window. What I saw amazed me. The roof of the house was covered with a deep layer of snow, and a huge snowdrift in the front yard came up to the eaves, hiding everything but a small area at the side of the house.

"I've been shoveling all week," Alan said, "and from the way it looks, Dad shoveled even more after I left."

"Wow, I don't think I've ever seen this much snow on the farm before," Mom said, looking around. "Look, it's up to the barn roof, and I can't even see the woodshed."

The front door of the house burst open and Grandma hurried out in her print dress and apron, waving her arms. Right behind strode Grandpa in a plaid shirt, his bald head uncovered, a big grin on his face, and a cigarette dangling from his mouth.

"Is he still on that medication?" Grandma asked as we clambered out of the car.

"No, his kindergarten teacher wrote a letter complaining about him not paying attention in class, and they took him off it," Mom replied.

"Well, thank God he's off that horrible stuff," Grandma said, patting me on the head. "We don't want you to miss Christmas, do we?"

I'd take back those effects, though, if that would have allowed me to miss the Christmas of 1950 at Grandma and Grandpa's house.

CHAPTER 24

A Not So Very Merry Christmas

Sunday morning started with a flurry of activities. Right after breakfast, Grandma started baking and cooking. Besides the four of us, Aunt Irene and her growing family and Aunt Rhoda were coming, making a grand total of seven adults and four children. Figuring out where everyone would sit in that small house was a test of Grandma's organizational skills.

Cutting down a tree a day or two before Christmas was a common practice at the farm because Grandma and Grandpa used candles instead of electric lights, and candles could easily start a fire. At breakfast the subject of a Christmas tree had come up, and Grandpa mentioned a little evergreen he had found while trekking through the woods one day. In response to this Grandma said, "Well, we need to get the tree up today, so if you think it's the right size, why don't you go out this morning after the chores are done and bring it in so we can get to trimming it."

"Yah sure, you betcha. I'll get to it right avay," replied

Grandpa, who was in his usual jovial mood. "I found a good vun. It's on da neighbor's land dhough. Vat do you tink?" he asked, winking at me. "Do you tink dey'll mind if ve use it fer avile?"

"Why would you get a tree from the neighbor's woods when we've got plenty of them in our own back yard?" Grandma asked.

"Because it's da right size and it's got da perfect shape. Hell, dey von't miss it, besides it's on our side of da road."

"Well, you do what you think is right," Grandma said, "but I want it put up this morning so we can trim it this afternoon."

[It's interesting how children pick up on the little things, and Grandpa's country values about cutting down a neighbor's tree certainly did not go unnoticed by me. To him, a tree in the middle of the great north woods was just another tree. That it happened to be on the neighbor's land meant nothing to him, but it was a value that did not, as I would later learn the hard way, fit life in the big city.]

Jean and I got busy helping Grandma make Christmas decorations, which consisted, as they always had, of popcorn strings, paper chains, and cutouts of snowflakes and angels. We started with the popcorn strings. As Larry was still too young to use a needle, Grandma gave him some toys to play with while Jean and I sat down at the kitchen table in front of a large bowl of popcorn. Because I was an old hand, I picked up the needle and thread that Grandma had prepared for me and got right to work. My string was halfway to the floor by the time Grandma finished showing Jean how to thread the popcorn.

"My string's bigger than yours," I bragged.

"So! I'm not racing you," she said, giving me that soulful look she always gave me when I challenged her.

I knew my sister. Contrary to her claim, I knew she would try her best to beat me. I reached into the bowl, picked up a handful of popcorn, placed it on the table in front of me, and quickly sorted through the pile to find the nice ones. The biggest kernels weren't always the best. I wanted to find plump ones with soft, fat centers, ones that wouldn't break apart when I slid the needle through them and that would take up plenty of space on my string.

We worked in silence. Sometimes Jean would say, "Oh, shoot!" when one of her kernels split into small pieces, but I stayed focused, and before I knew it my string was curled in a ball at my feet. Her string, I noticed, was still hanging only a foot off the edge of the table.

"Mine is already on the floor," I said smugly.

"I don't care," she said. "I'm not racing you, so there."

Larry, who had been playing on the floor by himself, stood up, and without saying a word, he rushed over and stomped on the string lying on the floor, breaking the kernels into small pieces and sending them flying in all directions.

"Grandma, Larry's ruining everything!" I shouted, looking down at the mess. Then Larry grabbed my string in the center and yanked. I hung on to the needle, but the string slid through the eyelet, sending what popcorn remained on the string flying in all directions.

Grandma grabbed Larry by the arm, but by that time it was too late. "Larry, go into the dining room right now," she said, pushing him toward the door. "I'll deal with you later."

"I hate you," I snarled, giving him a dirty look.

"I don't care, so ha, ha, ha," he said, and then he stuck his tongue out for good measure.

Grandma calmed me down and, restringing the needle, encouraged me to start over again. I did, but it wasn't the same. By this time, Jean's string was almost touching the floor and the bowl was two-thirds empty. Instead of making more popcorn, Grandma told us we would have to do with what we had, and then she went back to her cooking. When the bowl was empty, Grandma tied our strings together to make a long one, and then she cleared the table to make space for the other decorations.

The paper chains were simple to make. We cut red construction paper into small strips, curled them into circles, and glued the ends together with a paste that Grandma made from flour until we had two long chains. Then, just as she had done with the popcorn string, Grandma glued the two chains together.

The cutouts were more of a challenge. Grandma showed us how to fold a sheet of paper in half, cut holes around the edge, fold it again, and cut more holes. Like magic, when she unfolded the paper it resembled a snowflake. Well, Grandma's did, anyway. Some of mine looked more like snowballs.

The angels proved to be even more challenging. The bottom half was easy to make, but I had a heck of a time with the head, which was either too large or too small, and the arms, which were never the same size. Jean definitely beat me in the paper cutout contest.

When we were done we moved to the dining room where Mom was busy setting the table. After a few minutes, she told us to put our winter clothes on and go outside. Evidently she had had enough of our pent-up energy trying to break loose. Jean wanted to stay inside to help set the table, so Larry and I, our little spat forgotten, put on our winter duds and out we went.

It was cold and windy outside, and except for pulling each

other around on the sled, there wasn't much to do. I pulled Larry around the yard until my arms and legs got tired, and he made a valiant effort to pull me, but he was still too young, so it didn't take long before we gave up and moved back inside. As I recall, getting our winter clothes on and off took more time than we had spent outdoors.

Shortly after that, Grandpa arrived with our Christmas tree. It didn't take long for him to set it up because he had already nailed birch branches to the base of the tree to form a rough-looking stand. As he had promised, the tree was flawless. The branches were full and uniform in size, forming a perfect inverted V, and the top almost touched the ceiling.

Jean and I helped put the decorations on, and Mom lifted me up so I could put the angel on the top branch. Mom helped Grandma put on the candles, which were set in little silver holders that clipped to the branches. The holders looked like little teacups with a silver sidepiece that kept the flame from coming into contact with the tree. The reflection of the flame off the silver created a halo effect that modern lighting has tried, but failed, to duplicate.

"What is this for?" I asked, pointing at a pail of sand sitting next to the Christmas tree.

"That's in case of fire," Mom said.

I didn't understand what sand had to do with putting out a fire, but I was smart enough to know what could happen if a fire started in the living room or any other place in the house, for that matter. "Are we going to have a fire?" was the first thing that came out of my mouth.

"I hope not, but with candles you never know," Mom replied.

"What if a fire starts and we need to get out?" I asked, pointing toward the living room door, which was hidden somewhere behind the tree. I also knew that it was nailed shut, because when I had tried to open the door during our summer visit, it wouldn't budge. When I had asked Grandma about it, she said something about Grandpa nailing it shut because he didn't want anyone going in and out. The answer didn't satisfy my inquisitive nature, but it was as good as I would get from Grandma, who tired easily of my questioning ways. Why, at that young age, I was able to conceptualize the possibility of being trapped inside the house during a fire is a bit of a mystery, but I suspect that I had been taught about multiple fire escape routes at the orphanage or at school.

Before Mom could answer my question, Grandma said, with some irritation, "We never use that door anyway, and besides, we've been doing it this way ever since your mom was born, so let's not worry our little heads about a fire, OK? You kids go to the kitchen and I'll give you some milk and cookies."

That evening the family gathered around the dining room table. Grandpa lit his pipe, leaned his chair against the wall next to the potbellied stove, and watched in silence as we played cards and board games. We started with Old Maid and from there moved to Hearts, which proved to be a bit too much for Jean and me. After that, Mom pulled out the Chinese checkers board, which was quickly scrapped when we couldn't find some of the marbles.

"Let's play regular checkers!" I said eagerly.

"No, I don't want to," Jean said.

"Why? Because I always beat you?" I said with a smirk.

"No," she said, wrinkling up her nose. "I don't like it, that's all."

"We'll play one game of checkers," Mom said, "and then it'll be time for bed."

"I want black," I said, grabbing for the black checkers.

"I wanted black," Jean whined.

"Terry asked first," Mom said. "You can have black next time."

I lined up all of my checkers. Jean did the same on her side of the board, and we started playing. On that particular night, luck was on her side. When she jumped my last king, I tipped the board over, sending checkers flying all over the floor.

"Terry, that's not nice," Mom said.

"She cheated!" I said.

"I did not," said Jean, "I didn't cheat, Mom, he's lying."

"OK," Mom said, "this is a good time to stop. It's time for bed. You kids are going to have a big day tomorrow. Terry, pick up the checkers while I help your sister and brother brush their teeth. When you're done, come into the kitchen."

"No!" I snarled, putting my hands on my hips.

"Terry, you do as your mother said!" Grandma shouted from the kitchen, "or I'll get out the butter paddle and come in there. Do you want that?" I shook my head and climbed down from the chair. From the sound of her voice, I knew she was serious. Without another word, I picked up the pieces and put them back inside the box.

As we had on the previous night, Jean and I slept upstairs with Mom, and Larry slept in the Great Bed with Grandma and Grandpa. At around two or three in the morning, I felt someone shaking me, and I heard a voice say, "Terry! Wake up!"

I stirred, groaned, and pulled my knees closer to my chest. "Terry, wake up!" the voice said again, hands rocking me back and forth. "You had an accident!" An accident, I thought, still half asleep. I opened my eyes part way, yawned, and pulled the blanket over my face. I was warm and cozy and my nose was telling me the room was freezing cold.

"Get up!" the voice insisted. "I will not lay in your pee!" It was Mom. My eyes opened wide. No wonder I felt warm and cozy.

"What happened?" I heard Jean mumble.

"Get up. I have to change the sheets before it spreads into the mattress."

Jean and I rolled out of bed. We moved to a corner of the room and watched in silence as Mom changed the sheets. Within seconds, my entire body started to shake violently. In an effort to get warm, I crossed my arms over my chest and rocked back and forth, lifting one foot at a time in a futile attempt to keep my feet off the floor. When Mom was done, she changed my underwear as I continued to hop back and forth. "Stand still!" she said, "I can't get your underwear on if you keep moving your feet." I stopped rocking, stuck my foot into one of the holes, and almost jumped into the other. "You put your foot in the wrong hole," Mom said.

"I don't care," I said as I clambered back into bed, my underwear on backwards. Mom gave up in frustration. She pushed me towards the center of the bed and we snuggled for a few extra hours of sleep.

The next morning, Mom took the soiled sheets down to the kitchen, and as soon as Grandma saw us, she asked, "Did he wet the bed *too*? Your father is not very happy!" I could tell from the sound of her voice that it wasn't just Grandpa who was mad. "We'll make some new sleeping arrangements tonight," she said, "because we can't have this."

Mom and Grandma spent the morning cleaning and

preparing food for the expected company. To kill time, Jean, Larry, and I stood under the archway between the dining room and the family room and stared at the unlit tree, taking turns at guessing the contents of each package. From there we wandered over to the frosted dining room window, looking for signs of company. Tiring of that, we crowded into the kitchen, taking in the smells of Grandma's cooking, begging for sweets, and getting underfoot. When the adults tired of us, they shooed us out, and the cycle repeated itself.

Noon came and went with no sign of company. Outside, a never-ending blizzard raged. I heard the "clink, clink, clink" of the water dipper hitting the hand pump in the middle of the yard and also a high pitched whistle—probably the wind finding small openings in the side of the house.

Without a telephone at the farm, Dan and Irene could not communicate with us, and without a radio, it was impossible for us to know what the road conditions were like between Duluth and Cook. Finally, around two o'clock, Grandma said, "Let's go ahead and eat without them." By then, the food had cooled and everyone's mood was subdued. We had turkey, mashed potatoes, and homemade pumpkin pie. And of course there were leftovers, which we would be eating for the next week.

After the meal, we moved into the living room to open presents. We crowded around the Christmas tree, and Grandma carefully lit the candles, which quickly lit up the dreary and darkened room. She asked if we had learned any Christmas songs at the orphanage, and Jean and I struggled through *Jingle Bells*. After that, Grandma read *The Night Before Christmas* to us as we stared at the flickering candles on the tree.

When Mom had asked me what I wanted for Christmas, I

had told her a train set, not any old train set, but a locomotive with freight cars and a caboose that ran on tracks. Uncle Alan had one that he kept in his bedroom, and sometimes he would set it up on the dining room table and we would play with it. It made sounds just like a real train as it ran around on a track that curved around hills, through tunnels, and by houses and small towns, its horn tooting as it flew past crossroads. It never dawned on me that I had no place to put it, missing the obvious point that I couldn't bring it to the orphanage, but I had set my heart on getting one and that was that. The logistics were someone else's concern.

All that day, I had searched for a package big enough to have a train set inside, and seeing none, I had set my hopes on its arriving from Grandma and Grandpa's bedroom. Those quickly faded as Grandpa, instead of going to the bedroom, started handing out gifts. Larry's present that year escapes me, but I have a clear memory of Jean's. It was a rag doll with a large round face made out of thin, rigid plastic. It had long eyelashes, large eyes that opened and closed, freckles around a stubby nose, and fiery red hair made from cotton yarn. The plastic gave off a strong acidic odor that I can still smell. She still has that doll, stowed somewhere in her attic or basement.

I was visibly upset when Grandpa handed me the package with my name on it. Wrapped in colorful paper, the box was too small for a train set, so I set my sights on something else exciting. What that something else was, I didn't know, but I wasn't prepared for what I saw. I tore the wrapper off, and in my hands I held a plain-looking locomotive made out of wood. I looked at it for a few seconds, and then something inside me snapped. "That's stupid!" I shrieked, throwing it to the floor. "I wanted a *real* train, not that dumb thing!"

"I know that's not what you wanted, Terry," Mom said with a pained look, "but that's all I could afford. Maybe I can get you one next year."

Larry grabbed the train off the floor and said, "I'll have it!" Normally I would have fought with him, but I didn't bother. He could have it, as far as I was concerned.

I'm not sure what we did after the gifts had been opened. With all the leftovers, we probably had a late snack. I know I didn't get a lecture or the paddle for my outburst, although I deserved both for the pain I caused my mother. What had started out as a promising holiday had ended in disappointment for everyone. What I didn't know is that this was just the beginning of what would get even uglier.

CHAPTER 25
A Scarlet Holiday

On Christmas night, the outside temperature had dropped well below zero, and as Mom led us upstairs to bed, I could hear the wind howling and snow pelting the side of the house. The staircase to the second floor of the farmhouse was narrow and steep, and the outside wall, which was plastered and covered with faded and frayed green and tan wallpaper, stung the palm of my right hand as I pressed it against the wall for balance. Directly below the second-story window, the staircase took a ninety-degree turn. As I turned and walked up the final flight of steps, I felt a cold draft hit the exposed skin of my neck, sending a chill racing through my body. Five steps later, I was in the hallway.

The hallway was unadorned and dingy and not really a hallway at all but rather a quarter section of the upstairs that Grandpa never got around to finishing. The plastered walls to the bedrooms were unpainted and cracked, and in the spots where the plaster had fallen off, the underlying laths were showing. The overhead rafters were grayed with age and uncovered. In places, rusted shingle nails stuck through the roof boards, posing a danger to unsuspecting heads. Underfoot, scruffy, rough-hewn floorboards, many of which bowed in the center, created an uneven surface. The outside wall, starting at the base of the window and extending to the peak of the roof, was bare of anything save for the two-by-four studs that served as the frame for the house and the one-by-eight tongue-and-groove exterior pine boards that held everything together. On several of the boards, tin can tops covered holes where knots had fallen out. This was the exterior area of the house that Grandpa didn't get around to siding, so the only thing separating Larry and me from the blizzard raging outside were those thin pine boards.

Due to the accidents the previous night, Grandma elected to have Larry and me sleep on Army cots in the hallway. She must have told Grandpa to pull them out of storage during the day because they were already set up and waiting for us. With nothing else in the room and no guardrails around the opening to the staircase, the cots looked like two caskets sitting next to an open gravesite.

"Terry, why don't you take the cot in front, and Larry can have this one, " Mom said, pointing at the cot running parallel with the staircase. "Jean, you go into the bedroom and get ready for bed while I help the boys." Jean continued into the bedroom, leaving the door open so light from the lantern could filter in.

"It's cold," Larry moaned as he stripped to his shorts.

"It'll get warmer when you get under the covers," Mom said.

"No, it won't!" I complained. "There's no heat up here."

"I left the downstairs door open so the heat can come up the staircase," she said. "It might take a few minutes, but it'll get warmer."

"What if it doesn't?" I asked as I hurried to get under the green Army blanket that Mom had spread on the cot.

She didn't answer. Instead she said, "If you need to go to the bathroom, there's a five-gallon pail at the end of Larry's cot, and if you need more blankets, let me know."

"I need another blanket," I said, barely able to get the words out.

Mom put a second blanket over me and said, "There, does that help?"

"No! It's still cold."

"Well, that will have to do, because I don't have any more." Mom turned, went into the bedroom, and closed the door. A dim yellowish glow coming from the base of her door was enough to make out objects in the room, but when Mom extinguished the lantern, the hallway turned pitch black. Larry and I lay there listening to the sounds of the blizzard raging outside, feeling its wrath as it tried in vain to shake the house off its foundation. With every blow, the wooden legs of the Army cot vibrated, causing my head to jiggle on the pillow. Was the cot moving? I wondered. Would it fall into the dark hole and tumble down the staircase with me in it? After a while Larry whimpered, "I'm freezing."

"Tuck the blankets under you," I said, rolling back and forth in an effort to get part of them under me. I heard him toss back and forth trying to get comfortable until finally the noise stopped.

Sleeping on an Army cot in an unheated, uninsulated room is like sleeping on the sidewalk in the dead of winter. It's almost as hard as a sidewalk, and no matter how many blankets you have on top, it will always be cold underneath. I curled into a ball and managed to tuck some of the blankets under my body, but I never got completely comfortable.

I awoke in the early morning with an urge to pee. The wind had subsided and everything was quiet except for the ticking of the grandfather clock in the family room. My hips and back ached, and I felt a draft coming through the canvas of the cot. I contemplated my next move. Should I get out of bed and use the pail, or should I try to make it through the rest of the night? I thought about how cold I would be and how dark it was. Would I find the pail? Was it in the corner of the room or right at the foot of the bed? I couldn't remember. Should I holler for my mother? I'm not sure how long I lay there in indecision, but eventually nature took its course and I fell asleep feeling warm and cozy for the first time that night.

"Terry, it's time to get up," I heard a voice say from some-where above me. Slowly I opened the lids of my eyes. The early morning light streaming through the window almost blinded me, and then I saw Mom standing over me.

"What time is it?" I asked, my body frozen into a ball.

"It's time to get up. Grandma is downstairs getting breakfast ready and the men are already outside doing chores."

"I'm cold," I said, watching my breath hang like a cloud in front of my face.

"I can tell," she said, "your lips are blue, but if you hurry you can stand by the stove and get all warmed up. Larry, you too! You don't want to miss breakfast, do you?"

Larry bounded out of bed and ran down the steps, with Mom close behind.

I threw my covers off and sat up. As I started to stand up, I felt a burning sensation, and something tugged at my hip. Looking down, I saw a chunk of yellowish ice the size of a small plate clinging to the side of my underwear. I tried to pull it off, but it was embedded into the fabric. "Mom, where are my clothes?" I yelled.

"They're down here in the suitcase," she yelled back. "You can get dressed in the dining room by the stove."

Out of options, I went downstairs. As soon as I walked into the kitchen, Larry shouted, "Look, there's ice hanging on Terry's underwear." Going down on his haunches and pointing at me, he started to laugh.

"Eileen." Grandma said. "Take your son into the dining room and get him dressed. He can't come to the table in that condition."

How long Larry and I slept on the cots in the hallway is unclear, but I do know that Grandma kept the dining room door open all day in an attempt to heat the upstairs, so it was probably more than that one night. Within days, I got a sore throat, followed by a cold, which evolved into a fever. Larry also got sick, and at some point, they moved us from the hallway to the dining room. By this time, I had a rash and a high temperature and both of us were bedridden. For days, we lay in front of the potbellied stove with blankets wrapped around us. At night, Grandma or Grandpa would get up, put logs in the stove and, if we were awake, ask how we were doing. Our diet consisted of aspirin, cod liver oil, and chicken broth. The aspirin wasn't a problem for me, but I hated the cod liver oil. In Grandma's eyes, cod liver oil cured everything. I think she would have used it to mend a broken bone, given the chance.

One day Mom said, "Terry, I know getting sick isn't funny, but I have to tell you, you look like a clown."

It took a few moments for what she said to register because by this time I was physically weak and mentally drained, but when it did, I asked, "Can I see in the mirror?"

Mom carried me to the small mirror on the dining room wall and I looked in astonishment at my reflection. With the exception of an area circling my mouth, my face was beet red. The area around my mouth was white—not pale skin-tone white, but bright white. It looked like someone had painted clown makeup on my face. It started under my nose, circled my mouth, and went down almost to the bottom of my chin.

"How come I look like that?" I asked.

"I don't know, honey, but I'm sure Grandma's cod liver oil and lots of rest will clear it up."

It didn't, of course. Despite the home remedies, our condition got worse. Based on the date of our admittance to the hospital in Duluth, we may have been at the farm for up to two weeks before they made the decision to return us to the Children's Home. Why they didn't take Larry and me to the hospital in Cook or straight to the hospital in Duluth is perplexing at best and certainly inappropriate, given the seriousness of our condition.

On the day we left, Mom wrapped me in blankets and Uncle Alan carried me out to the car. Grandma came out of the house carrying something red and flaccid. "Here's a hot water bottle for Terry," she said. Mom put it on my lap under my blanket. Jean sat across from me in the back seat and I believe that Mom held Larry on her lap in the front, but I don't know if Grandma gave Larry a hot water bottle. I didn't have enough energy to move. I slouched against the door, my eyes closed. During the long ride to Duluth, everything went black—I saw thousands of stars floating at me from behind closed eyelids, and twice I had to throw up. Both times Uncle Alan stopped the car and opened the door, and I let it fly, narrowly missing the seat.

How the staff at the Children's Home reacted upon seeing Larry and me in that condition is unknown, and how long we stayed there before they took us to the hospital is also unknown, because I was totally out of it by that time. St. Mary's Hospital admitted us on January 9, 1951. The diagnosis was scarlet fever, which has been responsible for the deaths of many children over the centuries.

[During the nineteenth century, scarlet fever epidemics in the United States killed thousands of children. By the middle of the twentieth century it had pretty much been eradicated on an epidemic scale, but if not treated properly, it can still kill, and in our case, it almost did.]

A nurse in the hospital told me that Larry and I had one of the worst cases of the fever she had ever seen, and we were lucky to be alive. Personally, I don't think luck had anything to do with it. I think someone or something was looking over us and it wasn't Grandma. I had this gut feeling then and I still do, that Grandma subconsciously wanted Larry and me out of the way. I know that sounds terrible, but there you have it. I would see Grandma at least two more time but things were never the same—I had changed. Before the orphanage, I had had an alluring personality. Small for my age and cute, with two large dimples and thick, blond hair, I could win over anyone with my smile and charm. After the trauma of separation, the stay at the hospital as a "severe disciplinary case," and the near-death bout with scarlet fever, I had lost my innocence and trust. I had this sense that everyone and everything was against me. I was angry. I still have scars, both internal and external, from those days, scars I will most likely take with me to the grave.

Despite this (or perhaps due to this?) the next few years would not be as dramatic as the previous nine months. There would be other challenges, but I would gradually adapt and settle into a routine. At least I would have a place to call home and warm clothes. And, although the food wasn't as tasty as Grandma's, I would have plenty of it.

*"What goes up must come down, observed Pete, Duluth's Red Feather Kid, as he helps the small fry at Duluth Children's Home manipulate the teeter-totter.."***Duluth Harold staff photo**

CHAPTER 26

Orphaned

From day one, Mom's visits had been irregular, and it got worse after the scarlet fever incident. Mom had always relied on Uncle Alan or Dan for transportation. Alan, of course, came down from Cook only for special occasions, but Dan and Irene lived in Duluth, so Mom counted on Dan the most. If he wasn't available, Mom would take the city bus to within a few blocks of the Home and we would go with her for the day for picnics, shopping, or to the zoo, and return in time for her to catch the last bus back to wherever it was she lived. She never talked about her job, or where she lived, and I never asked.

Whenever Dan picked us up, we stayed at his house or we went to Grandma and Grandpa's farm. I enjoyed the trips to the farm, but I didn't like going to Dan and Irene's. Instead of spending time with us, Mom spent most of her time talking to Irene while we played by ourselves. I also didn't like to be around Uncle Dan. When he drank, which seemed to be all the time, he got loud and obnoxious, and he criticized everybody, including me, if the mood hit him. One time I heard him bellow, "That boy of yours isn't growing very fast, is he, Eileen, and he's looking more and more and more like that no-good husband of yours." He took no notice of my presence—it was as if I didn't exist or matter.

Irene said, "Dan, why do you say things like that? He has it tough enough without you criticizing him."

"Oh, I'm *sorry*," he said sarcastically. "He's a *big* boy now and he doesn't look *at all* like his dad. How's that!"

Larry, on the other hand, seemed to enjoy the weekends at Dan and Irene's. He and their youngest son, were the same age, so they played together. Jean and I had to find our own things to do. It was easy for Jean because she had a great imagination, especially when it came to dolls. She could sit in the corner for hours giving them instructions, changing their diapers, serving them meals, or pushing them around in a stroller. If Jean asked me to play house and I agreed, it was because I had nothing better to do. However, those moments didn't last long. As soon as Jean included me in the dialog with one of her dolls, saying, "Ellen, say hi to your Daddy," or "Terry, would you like to feed Sally?" I would run out of the room. Usually I could be found by myself riding the tricycle up and down the sidewalk, which by this time was about as exciting as making my bed.

On the way back to the orphanage Mom would stop at a corner grocery store so we could pick out treats. Candy cigarettes were Larry's and my favorite. It was a common sight to see people with cigarettes hanging out of their mouth, so we thought it was cool to pretend that we were smoking too.

During the summer of 1951, we spent an entire week at Grandma and Grandpa's farm. Dan drove, and on the way he stopped at a roadside store where Mom bought each of us cow-boy hats and sunglasses and, after some pleading, a Western magazine with pictures of horses and cowboys. I couldn't read, but the pictures appealed to me. All that week I dreamed of standing on a ridge in a field of tall grass with my horse next to me looking down onto a flat prairie that stretched as far as the eye could see.

[In my teens I would have another extended dream about a far off place across a great ocean, and like this dream, it too would be a glimpse into my future.]

Uncle Alan brought us back to Duluth the following weekend, and although I didn't know it at the time, that week would be the last time I would visit the farm.

Mom didn't spend much time at the orphanage, not like other moms. Even a dad who dropped his three children off every morning took the time to stay and visit. Parents were encouraged to drop in for holiday meals, especially during Easter and Christmas, but Mom didn't eat with us, and she never bothered to see my room, even after I offered to show it to her.

Gradually her visits became even less frequent. What had started out as every other week turned into once a month, and she even missed a few months. Once, after calling the Home to make the necessary arrangements, she failed to show. We wasted the entire morning waiting on the veranda. In the beginning I had been excited to see her, but as time dragged on the excitement turned into indifference, until finally I began to wish that she wouldn't come at all. We had friends by that time and an established routine with lots of activities.

CHAPTER 27

Mrs. Scheidler's Private Boarding School

In 2008 I interviewed a woman who had worked at the Children's Home while we were living there. She told me that Mrs. Scheidler ran the home like a "private boarding school." I got the impression from our conversation, that some of the staff members, especially those with degrees in the social sciences, found it difficult to work under her supervision and that her nineteenth-century approach to training and discipline caused some friction within the ranks.

Mrs. Scheidler's educational program started with proper table etiquette. She would invite a woman from her social circle to give us instructions. We were taught the different types and uses of forks and spoons and how to set a table and fold a napkin. We even had a lesson on how to curtsy and bow, which was somewhat confusing to me. Was I, upon meeting one of the girls in the hallway, supposed to bow, and would she in turn curtsy? The application would reveal itself later.

In one lesson our instructor asked an older boy to show us

how to escort a lady to the table. The boy, who obviously had done this before, walked over to a girl and said, "May I escort you to the table?"

Taking his arm, she said, "Yes, you may."

The boy gestured to a dining chair. "May I?"

"Yes, you may. Thank you."

He then pulled out her chair and she said, "Thank you so much."

"Excellent!" the lady said. "Now I want everyone to try it. Pick a partner and escort them to the table."

Total bedlam broke out. Several boys pulled the chairs out from under their partners, and then everyone else followed suit. I can still hear the lady shouting, "Stop this! Boys and girls, this is not funny! Stop it now!" but no one paid any attention until Mrs. Scheidler came in and put a stop to the free-for-all.

The boarding school mindset was most evident during the evening meal. Before the girls could come to supper they had to clean up and put on dresses, which for them meant two quick changes; when they returned from school they changed into their play clothes, and a hour later they had to put on a dress. The boys had it somewhat easier; we just had to wash our hands and faces. Then, as we walked into the dining room, a matron would inspect us. She checked our clothes, our finger-nails, and even behind our ears. If anything was out of place, we were sent back to our dorm to correct the problem.

Mrs. Scheidler was a fanatic about making us eat everything on our trays, and we didn't have a choice about what and how much because the kitchen staff doled out the food. "The boys and girls in India are starving," she would say, "so I don't want to see any food left!" To make matters worse, a staff member would inspect our trays at the end of each meal. If there was anything left, we had to sit at the table until it was gone. If we refused, we were sent to bed for the rest of the day, which was torture for a boy with my energy. Not only did I have to take off my clothes and get into bed, but also I had to lie there for hours listening as the other children played outside. I went through this only once. After that, I made up my mind: inedible food, food unfit for human consumption—usually vegetables—would go into my pocket and afterwards, be flushed down the toilet.

I especially hated rutabagas. Just looking at them made me gag. Getting them into my pocket, I quickly learned, was a challenge. First, there was the problem of getting caught, and second, if I squeezed too hard, the rutabagas turned into mush before they even got there. The solution, I learned, was to wait until almost everyone had gone. I would then kneel on my chair, and after a quick check to make sure no one was looking, I would grab a handful of rutabagas and carefully drop them in. Afterwards I would go to the downstairs bathroom and empty my pocket in the toilet. Maybe that's why my pockets were always so stiff, even after washing.

Square dancing was also included on Mrs. Scheidler's list of favorite things to do. An announcement would be made at mealtime that everyone was expected to participate in square dancing that afternoon, and we would all file down to the playroom in the basement. The boys would stand against one wall and the girls the other. Then, with Mr. Kolander calling and Mr. Jensen playing the fiddle, we would make fools of ourselves as we traipsed around in circles to the music. This is where the formal training on genuflection came to good use. We would approach a girl, bow, and ask, "May I have this dance, please?" The girl would then curtsy and say, "I would love to. Thank you."

"Cleanliness is next to godliness" is a cliché Mrs. Scheidler repeatedly cited during her training sessions, and she backed it with action. Our clothes were always clean and everyone took a bath once a week. I washed myself with a washcloth every morning, or at least whenever I wet the bed. Coming from a family that wore their clothes until they dropped off and who took baths in a pail with hard water and lye soap, I didn't object to this new lifestyle. In fact, I adopted it immediately and without fuss.

If these old-fashioned traditions were the main cause of the conflict between Mrs. Scheidler and the staff, I would have to side with Mrs. Scheidler, but I don't believe that's the case. I believe it went much deeper, but to get there, it's important to understand the role of the staff.

CHAPTER 28
No Hugs Allowed

I never got close to any of the men and women who worked at the Children's Home, which, as it turns out, was the result of policy rather than staff indifference. The woman I interviewed in 2008 told me that Mrs. Scheidler continually warned the staff about not becoming too attached to the children because this would cause additional separation anxiety when the child left. She also wrote me a nice letter that says, "It [the Children's Home] was a safe, secure refuge...but it still was not home," with the comment, "I feel the same way about being in assisted living!"

Apart from this lack of affection, I have always felt that the staff, on the whole, were decent and caring men and women who did their best to make life easier for me and for the other children, and at no time was I physically abused. The manner in which Mrs. Scheidler ran the Home was strange, but not really offensive. Fairness, however, was an emotional issue for me, one that continues to this day. Sometimes I was disciplined for a misdeed I had not done, and what disturbed me the most about that was the lack of any effort by staff to get to the bottom of what happened. In addition, some of the discipline handed out might be unacceptable by today's standards.

The sleeping and living arrangements at the Home were segregated by age and gender. The babies and toddlers of both sexes occupied the second floor. The older boys occupied the third floor, and the older girls lived in a residential house across the parking lot from the main building. Each accommodation had a supervisor, an assistant supervisor, and matrons who worked the night shift. According to an old pay ledger, the staff also included a full-time nurse, a cook, cleaning ladies, a laundress, a dining room girl, a bookkeeper, a maintenance man, a caseworker, and a seamstress. At various times during my stay I had contact with all of them, but only a few remain firmly implanted in my memory.

Miss Kelly, the second floor supervisor and full time resident, was the only woman on the second floor whom I knew by name. That was because she was the youngest and the prettiest and she went out of her way to be nice. She would always greet me with a "Hi, Terry, how *are* you?" If I asked her to help me with something, like pinning up my snow pants or tying my shoelaces, she would stop what she was doing and come to my rescue. Once during dinner when I was having a difficult time eating my vegetables, she came to my table and said, "Are you OK, Terry?"

"I can't eat these," I said. "They make me throw up."

"Are you sick?"

"No. I just can't eat them."

She took my tray, winked, and said, "I'll take your tray to the kitchen. You run along and play."

Mr. Kolander replaced Mrs. Knutson as the supervisor of the third floor. I'm not sure when this changeover took place, but he was there when I returned from my bout with scarlet fever. Like Miss Kelly, Mr. Kolander made a lasting impression on me, but unlike her, I didn't trust him, and for this reason I never went to him for help unless it was absolutely necessary. He didn't abuse me, but to me he seemed to lack empathy for the boys under his care, and he made snap judgments, and that upset me. He was a large burly man, with short-cropped hair and a boyish face. Someone once told me he had worked his way through college as a lumberjack, which would explain the checkered red and black wool shirts he always wore. However, it wasn't until one warm summer afternoon in 1951 that I had my first real run-in with Mr. Kolander.

On the day in question, I left the Children's Home by the front door. My intent was to go down to Chester Park. As I crossed over Fifteenth Avenue, I noticed that some of the other children from the orphanage were at the park, and then I spotted the two older Williams brothers. I had seen the brothers many times, especially during the winter at the hockey rink, and I knew they lived right next to the girls' house, but I had never talked to them and I didn't know their first names. They were the only neighborhood boys who spent a lot of time on the playground. [Tommy Williams would later go on to play professional hockey, including a short stint with the Minnesota North Stars.] I could hear the brothers taunting the children and then I saw them throwing rocks at each other. They were standing about forty or fifty yards apart, essentially creating an obstacle course for anyone who might want to go from one side of the playground to the other. I'm not sure how it all started, but I could tell from the tone of their taunting that it was malicious and it was directed at the other children. They were daring them to run between them. As they say, life is about choices, and I had a choice to make. I could walk around them, but that was out of my way and, I reasoned, it would make their day, so I took off running. As I crossed between them, a rock struck me solidly on the right side of the head. I went down to my knees and I put my hand on my head. When I pulled it away, I saw blood on my fingers. Several of the children from the orphanage ran to my aid while one of the girls ran to fetch an adult. Within minutes, Mr. Kolander showed up.

"What's going on here?" he demanded.

The children told him what they had seen, and some of them even pointed at the Williams house. After gathering what he thought were the facts, Mr. Kolander grabbed me by the ear and wordlessly pulled me all the way to the nurse's office, where my wound was cleaned and bandaged. Then he confined me to my room for the rest of the day. From then on I stayed as clear of him as I could, and I never trusted him again. It didn't dawn on me at the time that Mr. Kolander wasn't in a position to discipline the Williams brothers.

The only other staff member who left an impression was the seamstress, Mrs. Miller. She was a gentle, soft-spoken woman with a full head of pure white hair. Whenever I needed something mended, such as a hole in the knees of my pants or a missing button, I would find Mrs. Miller. Sometimes she didn't even bother to ask me to take off my clothes, so every once in a while she would accidentally prick me with her needle. When I'd jump, she'd say, "Terry, stand still. A little needle prick never hurt anyone."

Besides mending clothes, Mrs. Miller helped at the girls' house and, since she had been a nurse in her youth, assisted the full time nurse with some of her duties. In fact, I probably wouldn't have remembered her if not for the shots. It was Mrs. Miller who gave me one of the triple vaccine shots—the one in the butt. I can still see her white hair as she said, "Take your pants down and bend over my knee, Terry. I promise, you won't feel a thing." Between mending clothes and giving shots, Mrs. Miller had a thing for needles. I wanted to stick her, to see how she liked it, and I wasn't the only one who felt that way.

Like I said, my experience with the staff was, by and large, a good one. They made my stay tolerable, if not enjoyable. I learned to respect authority, to be independent, and to be responsible for my actions. However, they did have to administer Mrs. Scheidler's discipline policies, which I suspect was the real cause of the conflict between her and the staff , and I felt the sting of many of those policies.

CHAPTER 29
The Sting of Discipline

Mrs. Scheidler's affection for nineteenth-century traditions included disciplinary practices that some today might consider antiquated, although I've run into some people who strongly believe we need to go back to some of those traditions. I, for one, breathed a sigh of relief when change finally arrived, but without first experiencing those traditions, I would have had no basis of comparison.

Most of the infractions I witnessed while I was at the orphanage were minor, like running in the hallways, talking back, or not obeying orders. Some, like fighting, were more serious. Theft was almost unheard of, but I do recall one incident involving Mr. Kolander that caused a fair amount of attention. He accused a boy on the third floor of stealing an unidentified item from his room. When a search of the boy's footlocker failed to find the item and when no one stepped forward with information, Mr. Kolander confined everyone on the third floor to the dorm for the rest of the day. This did not affect me, because I didn't sleep in the dorm. I heard later that Mr. Kolander found the item in his room, but of course by then it was too late to take the punishment back. As far as I know, he never apologized.

Public humiliation was the preferred punishment. For meal-time disobedience, like throwing food or acting out, violators had to sit in an oversized highchair at the head of the dining room tables wearing a cone-shaped dunce hat. During the meal, the other children taunted the offender with little, if any, censure from the adults.

I made several visits to the infamous chair, but only one stands out. It was the first warm day of the year, and with my chores done, I was eager to play outdoors. I don't remember the rule I broke, but it must have been a good one because, if memory serves me correctly, I had been a permanent resident for some time before the incident occurred. The noon meal that day was chicken, mashed potatoes and gravy, canned pears, and the most hated of all foods, rutabagas. I ate quickly, leaving the rutabagas for last. As usual, I waited until the end of the meal to try to shove them into my pocket. But the highchair presented a real problem: the space between its tray and my lap was so tight that I had trouble just getting my hand under the tray, let alone into my pocket. To make matters worse, I was sitting at the head of the room where everyone could plainly see me.

Determined not to eat the hated white vegetable, I looked around, and when no one was watching, I threw a piece at the garbage can by the kitchen door. I missed and it landed on the floor. I tried and missed again. At this rate, I thought, the floor around the garbage can would look like Grandpa's yard before I could empty the tray, and sooner or later someone was bound to catch me.

Trapped, I finally decided that I had no choice—I had to eat them. The first gag came before I could even lift the spoon off the tray. It started in my stomach and expanded upward until it came out of my mouth as a muffled belch, my upper torso convulsing violently. Fighting back another convulsion, I forced a spoonful into my mouth. Then, with my mouth still open, I spooned in more, and finally swallowed. This triggered another convulsion, and another, as I kept shoveling the ruta-bagas down my throat. When I had just one spoonful left, the convulsion turned into an eruption. Everything came spewing out, filling my tray with a white lake of chicken, mashed pota-toes, pears, and chunks of rutabagas.

I sat there staring at the pasty white puke, sweat beads on my forehead, palms wet with perspiration, chest aching from the contractions. Taking a deep breath, I looked around to see if anyone had been looking, and to my relief, I saw that most of the children had already left and the few remaining adults were deep in conversation. I looked at the tray again and considered my options: If I left it in that condition, I would be confined to my bed for the rest of the day, and I certainly couldn't *hide* the mess, so the only practical option was to eat it.

This time, instead of using my spoon, I lifted the tray to my mouth and drank the lumpy mixture as quickly as I could. It went down astoundingly well, considering what had just hap-pened, and I didn't go into any more convulsions. With my tray clean, or at least as clean as a tray can get without being licked, I raised my hand for permission to leave. One of the matrons came over and unfastened me, and I slid to the floor and ran upstairs. I can still see the granular residue on the tray left by the mashed potatoes and white rivulets of thicker particles that reminded me of the tributaries of a river.

For other infractions, like talking back or not doing what we were told, we had to stand in a corner or, if we were really bad, behind the front door. The door, which was mainly glass, had a latch that fastened to the inside wall. When fastened, it created a triangular space between the door and the corner of the wall. It was a perfect cage for little boys who didn't behave.

I know that I spent my share of time behind that door. I recall the time a mother and daughter walked past me on the way to Mrs. Scheidler's office. The girl pointed at me and asked, "Mom, what's that boy doing behind there?"

"Don't pay any attention to him," her mother said. "He's probably being punished for something." The girl smiled at me, but the smile turned into a frown when I gave her the tongue.

An hour later, I watched in stunned silence as the poor girl clung to her mother's leg, screaming, "Please don't leave me here, Mom! I'll behave, I promise! I'll do everything you tell me." It took two matrons to pull her free, and I heard her screaming all the way up to the second floor.

[Children being torn from their mothers was a common sight at the Children's Home. Day care centers have the same problem, but the atmosphere at the orphanage made such transitions more difficult. It looked and felt like an institution, not a playground or activity center, and there wasn't that, "I'll pick you up in the afternoon, honey," kind of goodbye that children quickly learn to trust. The goodbyes at the orphanage sounded hopeless: "It won't be for long," or "I'll be back when I can."]

Whenever two boys were caught scuffling, Mr. Kolander would drag them to the basement. There they would duke it out with boxing gloves until either blood was drawn or one of the boys went down. Most of my tussles were over almost before they began, so I didn't consider them real fights, and no one caught us. One, however, did end in a trip to the basement.

Toby and I had become friends because, like me, he didn't fit in. My isolation was self-imposed, but Toby's was because of his weight and his thick glasses, one of which had a cracked lens. The older boys teased him and called him Tubby, Fatso, Tub of Lard, or Four Eyes. I just called him Toby, and I felt sorry for him.

One afternoon, Toby and I were playing with our toy trucks in the dirt by the front entrance when Steven decided to butt in.

"Hey, Tubby, let me have your truck!" Steven demanded.

Toby bowed his head, ignoring Steven.

"Did you hear me, Fatso? Let me have your truck!"

"He doesn't have to give you his truck," I said, "We're playing with them. Why don't you go and get your own?"

"Because I don't want to, stupid! Stay out of this or I'll beat you up."

Steven reached down and grabbed the truck from Toby's hands, and instead of walking away, he pushed Toby into the dirt. "Thanks, Fatty," he said.

I grabbed for the truck and a struggle ensued. I don't know how long we wrestled, but eventually Steven got control. Just as he was about to strike me with the truck, Mr. Kolander intervened. "What's going on here? You know what happens when I catch anyone fighting. Let's go!" and with that, he grabbed both of us by our earlobes. When we got to the basement, Mr. Kolander helped both of us into boxing gloves. They were obviously made for an adult, because they came up to my elbows. Just keeping my arms raised took some effort. Mr. Kolander explained the rules. "This is how we solve our differences around here, not out in the hallway or on the playground. I won't stop the fight unless I feel that one of you will get injured. Is that understood?"

The room was now packed with boys who had come to witness the spectacle. Steven and I stared at each other for what seemed like an eternity. Finally Mr. Kolander said, "Well, you wanted to fight. What are you waiting for? Fight!" The room erupted with muffled shouts and encouragements from the other boys. "Beat him up, Terry!" "Knock him down!"

Steven landed the first punch, to my ear. For a split second I was stunned, but I quickly recovered and landed a right to the side of his head. We didn't do any rope-a-dope or fancy footwork; we just kept swinging. Sometimes a punch would connect, but more often than not, we just hit each other's gloves. Once Mr. Kolander stopped the fight to put one of my gloves back on. It had flown off when I threw a roundhouse and my arm had connected with Steven's. I'm not sure how long the fight lasted, but throughout it my teeth were clenched and tears were streaming down my face. Toward the end my arms felt like lead. But I never stopped, or maybe I should say, I couldn't stop. It's a trait that would follow me throughout life, one that became my trademark—keep going until you drop or your opponent drops, whichever comes first, and it was never me. Steven finally went to the mat, to use a boxing term. I don't know if I knocked him down or if he just gave up. I suspect the latter because I seriously doubt that I landed a punch with enough force to deck him. I would see him in the halls or at mealtime after that, but we never talked about what happened, and he never bothered me again. I learned some valuable things about myself during that fight, things that I would use on many occasions over the years.

During the winter of 1951, Mrs. Scheidler suddenly vanished. She didn't say goodbye and there was no farewell speech or gathering. She was there one day and gone the next. The woman I spoke to in 2008, told me that she died of cancer. With her departure, many of her "boarding school" policies vanished, and everyone seemed to breathe a sigh of relief.

CHAPTER 30
Candy Money

I don't recall the year I got my first job but I do know how it happened. One Saturday, I was sitting on the bench in the lobby after breakfast, blowing smoke rings into the air. They weren't really smoke rings, but it was so cold in the lobby that when I forced my breath out like I had seen adults do with cigarette smoke, a donut-shaped cloud would form in front of my face. Without warning. Mr. Kolander appeared at my side. "Terry, you're just the young man I was looking for."

Startled, I replied, "What did I do?" thinking, of course, that I had done something wrong.

"Well, as far as I know you didn't do anything. I was wondering if you would like to earn some money."

"Money?" The idea had never occurred to me before, but now it piqued my curiosity. I had seen some of the older boys doing chores on weekends, but it had never dawned on me that they might be getting money for it. "Can I buy candy with it?"

"You can buy anything you want, or you can put it in the

office safe, but you have to earn it first. Do you think you're big enough to work like the older boys?"

"Yes! What do I have to do?"

"Do you know where the pail and mops are in the basement?"

"Uh-huh."

"Well, you go get one of the pails and fill it with water. It doesn't have to be full—half is fine. When you've done that, bring the pail and one of the mops to me. I'll be waiting right here. Do you think you can do that?"

"Uh-huh!" I said, nodding my head in excitement as I headed for the basement.

Five minutes later, I returned with the mop and pail. "Now what do I do?"

"What I'd like you to do is wash these stairs."

"All the way to the top?" I asked, now beginning to regret the idea. There had to be at least a gazillion steps.

"No, only up to the second floor. One of the other boys is already cleaning the steps from the second to the third floor."

I stared at the steps. This was going to seriously cut into my playtime. "How long will it take?"

"If you piddle around it will take a while. But if you buckle down, it shouldn't take more than an hour. There are only about twenty steps, plus the landing."

He showed me how the mop and bucket with the squeeze thingamabob worked. It was quite simple, actually. He put the mop in the water and pumped it up and down, just like Grandma used to do when she churned butter. Then he put it between some rollers and pulled it out, clean and ready to go. After a few tries I got the hang of it. The hard part was walking up and down the steps to clean the mop because the bucket was too big to carry up and down. The whole job took a little over an hour, which wasn't bad for the first time. As I got better at it, I was able to finish in less than an hour. The pay wasn't good, but it was enough to buy candy, and I actually put most of the money into the superintendent's safe. I still have some of those coins, and even now I don't like to spend more than I make. I have always been emotionally driven to save for a rainy day.

CHAPTER 31
Handouts and Old Shoes

The orphanage provided clothing and shoes for children who didn't get what they needed from their parents. During the first year of our stay at the Home, Mom would bring us to the Salvation Army for clothes but I don't recall her ever getting each of us more than one item at a time and that was usually seasonal. As summer was approaching, it might be a short-sleeved shirt for Larry and me, and maybe a dress for Jean. As winter was approaching, it might be mittens or earmuffs. As her visits started to become more and more infrequent, this practice stopped. From that point on, we relied on the orphanage for all of our clothes. If I needed a pair of pants or a shirt, one of the floor matrons would escort me to the Clothes Closet, where I got to try on the item before it was assigned to me.

It wasn't really a closet, it was a room on the second floor with a sign on the door that read: "Clothes Closet." I distinctly remember the overpowering scent of fresh clothes and the deathly quietness of the room. Some of the clothes hung on racks, others were on shelves, and still others lay in piles on the floor. Due to my short stature, the matron would usually direct me to one of the piles while she rummaged through the shelves. When one of us found something suitable, the matron would lay it on the counter and write my name on the label. This was the only way the women in the laundry knew who the clothes belonged to. Once, when a matron couldn't find the label, she wrote my name on the back of the inside pocket flap. When I asked her why it didn't have a label, she told me that sometimes the stores that donated the clothes cut them off to keep them from being resold. This puzzled me, but I let it go. I still have a green corduroy shirt and two pairs of pants from those days and my name and the labels are missing. I believe that someone at the Home cut the labels off to prevent me from remembering my last name. They did the same thing with a bible that belonged to me.

For some unknown reason, we didn't need permission to get shoes. They were crammed inside a long wooden box attached to the inside wall of the first floor veranda and free for the taking. Whenever we needed shoes, we could go to the box and rummage around until we found something we liked. If we were lucky, we might find a new pair, but most of the shoes were scuffed and worn. Some didn't even have laces or a mate.

One day, as I was rummaging through the box, I came across a pair of high-top boots. I had always wanted boots, and these were particularly nice because they were black with red stitching and they came all the way up to my calf. I sat on the cover of the bench and pulled them on. They were a little snug and the tongue bulged at the ankle, but I didn't care, I had to have them.

I enjoyed wearing the boots and I showed them off to my

friends. Then, maybe a month or so later, I felt a stinging sensation on the sole of my right foot as I walked to school. When I got to the classroom, I sat down at my desk, lifted my foot, and looked at the bottom of the boots. Sure enough, in the middle of the leather sole, there was a hole about the size of a quarter. I tried walking without shuffling and that helped somewhat, but when the sock wore through and my bare feet hit the cold sidewalk, I realized that I had to do something different. By that time, the sole on the second boot had given out. I'm not sure where the idea to put newspapers in the bottom of the boot came from, but it was a great idea and it worked. It worked, that is, until the snow came, and even then I would have kept wearing the boots if it hadn't been for one of the matrons. It happened when I returned from school during the first blizzard of the year. A matron who was helping children take off their winter clothes instructed me to take my boots. When I removed the first boot, the newspaper, which had frozen to my sock, fell to the floor.

"Terry, you have a hole in the bottom of your shoe! What about the other one?"

I stared at her, knowing that the jig was up. She would take my boots and I'd never see them again.

"It's all right." I said, "I don't mind."

"Well, you might not mind, but you can't be walking around with holes in your shoes! You'll freeze your feet off. Take your other shoe off and we'll go find you a new pair."

"They're boots!" I corrected her.

"Shoes, boots, what's the difference?" she said with a frown. "You can't go to school with holes in your soles. What will your teacher think of us?"

She took me out to the veranda, and after scrounging

through the box for a few minutes, she picked out a pair of ugly brown shoes with square toes. "Here, try these on," she said, "they look about the right size." The shoes fit, but I hated them.

In the spring, after the snow had melted, I went back to the veranda to see if I could find something else. To my surprise, there were the boots, sitting right on top of the pile. At first I thought someone had repaired the soles, but when I turned them over, the holes, like two black eyes, stared back at me. I threw the brown shoes in the box, and with the prize boots tucked under my arm, I snuck out of the veranda. Within the week, the same matron caught me, newspapers and all, and despite intense protesting, she took the boots away again. I never saw them after that, but I did end up with a nice pair of red and white canvas tennis shoes. I wore those shoes until the soles were smooth and my big toes were sticking out the front. Mom had made a point of dressing me in fashionable clothes when we lived in Morgan Park, but old habits are difficult to break.

CHAPTER 32
Dumb But Not Stupid

As far as I know, all of the school-aged children at the orphanage attended Endion Elementary School. Grade school was K-6, which means that most of the children were in the five- to twelve-year-old range. It's quite possible that a few of the children in the girl's cottage attended another school, but other than the one eighteen-year-old I ran into, I don't believe any of the boys on the third floor that were old enough for the higher grades.

[The old Endion School building still stands. It is now an apartment complex and the playground is a parking lot, but the exterior remains unchanged. Built in 1890 and designed by Adolph F. Rudolph, the structure typifies many Neo-Romanesque institutions erected in the United States during the late nineteenth and early twentieth centuries. With its massive walls, cathedral-like roofline, towers, and arched windows, it recalls the building styles of eleventh-century Europe.]

I didn't do well in school. The long stretches of time away

from school while I was in kindergarten put me behind in my studies, and the stress of watching my peers excel was more than I knew how to handle. I didn't have parents or a mentor to guide me, and the orphanage didn't seem to care. So instead of trying to catch up, I withdrew. I spent most of my classroom hours daydreaming about recess and after-school activities. It wasn't a total waste of time. By the end of second grade, I could tell time, count to one hundred, and do simple math, but I couldn't read or write. In the school record, my second grade teacher, Mrs. Hallberg, wrote, "Terry has a limited sight vocabulary and is unable to attack many new words independently because of his lack of phonetic understanding and application." In conclusion, she wrote, "By repeating the second grade next year, Terry will learn these skills and read with understanding and enjoyment." Putting it bluntly, I flunked second grade.

I don't remember Mrs. Hallberg, but her comments about my intellectual growth were prophetic. By the time I turned nine, I would be reading at, or above, my age level, and by the end of fourth grade I had finished reading *A Tale of Two Cities*. The love of reading continues to this day, for I am never without at least one open book, usually two, and audio books clutter the front seat of my car. It's one of the few activities at which I can multitask and the only one that brings with it a sense of pure enjoyment.

Mrs. Hallberg also evaluated my emotional growth. Other than the hospital record of my "Severe Disciplinary Case" in 1950, it is the only written documentation I have found that addresses the state of my emotions during those difficult times. The subheading under Emotional Growth reads, *to be self-confident, self-controlled, happy, and relaxed.* The objective was to assess my growth in those four categories. Mrs. Hallberg did not note any improvement. Instead, her assessment reads, "He is too self-confident and easily angered when not given his own way." She goes on to suggest that for growth to take place, "He must learn to conform to room regulations and appreciate the rights of others." In other words, she saw no emotional growth or, more accurately, she made a judgement of my "difficult" temperament as a warning signal to other teachers. What steps she took over the course of the school year to channel my emotions in the right direction are not addressed.

I can relate to the self-confidence Mrs. Hallberg saw in me, but in retrospect, what she considered *too self-confident*, I now consider insecurity. In other words, I compensated for my deep insecurity by acting overly confident. The anger she alludes to came from fear. In the classroom, it was the fear of looking stupid, but in a much broader sense, it was the fear of losing my sense of self-worth. At some point in my childhood, I learned to harness the power of anger as a means to an end: the end, of course, being self-preservation.

I believe that my poor start in school can, to a great extent, be attributed to the separation from my mother, the six months on Phenobarbital, and the bout with scarlet fever. The orphanage, however, also bears some responsibility as the boarding school protocol emphasized by Mrs. Scheidler did not extend to education. The Home did not provide a study room or study time. We couldn't go to our dorms during the day, other than to change our clothes, and we didn't have chairs, let alone tables, at which we could study. And without a backpack, carrying books the six blocks to and from school wasn't a practical option. The Home did have a small library in one corner of the entertainment room, but the books were mostly adult, and the door was locked during the week. In addition, the staff never took an interest in helping the children with homework. I don't recall Mr. Kolander, or any other staff member, for that matter, encouraging me to study or offering to help. Once I returned home from school, I was free to run and play with the other children, and that's what I did.

The walk to school continued to be stressful for me, and, in fact, the bad memories of that walk far outweigh any I have of the classroom. For instance, one morning, as I was approaching the intersection of the third block, I saw two of the older children from the girl's cottage standing in the middle of the sidewalk—perhaps twenty yards ahead of me. In front of them stood two neighborhood boys, their arms outstretched.

"Where do you think you're going?" one of the boys asked.

"We're going to school. Let us pass!" said one of the girls in a challenging tone.

"Not until you pay us," the other boy smirked.

"I'm not paying you anything! Get out of our way!" she said, and with that the girls pushed their way past without a scuffle.

I walked towards the boys, both of whom were bigger than me, hoping they would follow the girls to school, but to my chagrin, one of them turned and spotted me.

"Where do you think *you're* going?" he barked, his arms outstretched.

"To school."

"You have to pay us. Do you have any money?"

"No," I mumbled.

"Well, then you can't go by," they roared in unison.

"I can't be late, I'll get in trouble!" I pleaded.

"*We* don't care," said the boy closest to me, a note of sarcasm in his voice.

I looked at them for a second, and then I headed for the

grass with the intent of walking around them. As I did, one of the boys pushed me. I stumbled and fell to the ground, and the other boy rolled me onto my stomach. Then he sat on my back and spread my arms out while I struggled to free myself.

"You think you're tough!" the boy sneered.

"Yeah, you think you're tough," echoed the other boy as he towered over me. "We'll show you how tough you are!"

"What are you boys doing?" a female voice shouted from somewhere off in the distance.

"We're not hurting him, Mom," said the boy who was sitting on me. "We're just having a little fun."

"Get off him right now and come here!"

The boy got off and both of them ran toward the house. "I'm sorry, little boy," the mother shouted from her steps. "Why don't you run along now?" She grabbed each of the boys by an ear and dragged them into the house.

The entire incident had taken only a few minutes, but from that day on, whenever I would see the boys standing on the sidewalk, I would take the shortcut, or if I saw them walking towards school, I would hold back and follow at a safe distance. I used to joke that I may be dumb, but I'm not stupid, and that applied in this case. I had not yet learned the art of fighting, and even if I had, taking on two older boys would have been stupid. Walking to school tested my courage, but it didn't stop there—even the walk to Sunday school would prove to be as challenging, but in a different way.

CHAPTER 33

Tongue-tied

On Sundays, Jean and I would walk six blocks to the Covenant Church. A bus took Larry and most of the other children to the downtown Presbyterian Church. Why they split us up is unknown, but I recall Jean telling me once that Larry wanted to be with his friends, and evidently that was reason enough. Sunday school was fun. The boys and girls in our class didn't even know we were from the orphanage, or if they did, they never mentioned it. We seldom stayed for the church service. On those rare occasions when our class sang or performed for the congregation, Jean and I would participate and then leave by the side door instead of staying for the sermon.

On one particularly cold winter morning, Jean and I left the Children's Home for our weekly hike to Sunday school. Our boots made a crisp, crunching sound on the compacted snow, and our breaths froze in the air, disappearing only after another breath took its place. I looked up at the bright blue, cloudless sky, my mind wandering aimlessly. About halfway across the bridge over Chester Creek, I stopped to stare at the beauty of the surrounding scene. Ice completely covered the ordinarily fast-flowing river that snakes down from the bluffs overlooking the city. A fresh coat of snow blanketed the rocky, uneven cliffs on both sides of the creek bed and a thin layer of the white powder covered every tree branch as far as I could see. Even more stunning was the cloud of glistening crystals that hung over the entire area, giving it a truly otherworldly look and feel.

"Terry, what are you doing?" I heard Jean say from somewhere up ahead. "We're going to be late!"

Turning, I noticed that she was almost across the bridge and then, without answering, I walked over to where the sound of rushing water was coming from. I stepped onto the cement ledge, put my elbows on the metal railing, and bent forward to get a better view.

The scene was magical. Ice hung in sheets down the face of the waterfall, and at about midpoint it turned back into its liquid form, splashing into the half-frozen pool directly below me. Suspended above the waterfall was a small rainbow. Mesmerized, I leaned closer to the railing and, without thinking, stuck out my tongue.

It took only a fraction of a second to realize what I had done, but by then it was too late. The railing had my tongue and it was not about to let go. "Never, ever put your tongue on anything that's metal during the winter." How many times had I heard Grandpa say those words? Plenty, I bet.

Yelling for Jean, who by this time had retraced her steps and was now standing close to me, I mumbled, "Ell! Ah, uch!"

"What did you go and do that for?" she asked in that scolding tone she always used when I did something to disturb her comfort zone. It was the same tone our Grandma used when I did something dumb.

"EH EEEE!" I said, the words barely audible.

"What do you want me to do? This is stupid!" she spat, stomping her foot. "This is really stupid! Now we're going to be late for Sunday school."

"Uh UH!" Actually, I wanted to tell her to shut up.

"Should I run back to the Home and get help?"

"Ng, ng!" I said, vibrating my head back and forth in an effort to say no without ripping the tongue out of my throat.

"This is *really stupid*," she said for the third time.

"Eingh ungh ungh!" I tried to scream.

"Find someone? Should I go to the store across the street?"

I vibrated my head up and down to signal yes and she ran off. I couldn't move. My tongue was sticking out as far as it would go, and my mouth was wide open. A voice inside kept saying, "Keep your lips away from the railing. Keep your lips away from the railing." My jaw started to ache and I felt the metal's coldness radiate into my mouth and onto my lips. Then, after what seemed like forever, Jean returned.

"The man from the store is going to help," Jean said, leaning close to my face.

"Hi there, young man! I see you've got yourself in a little predicament! Don't move. I'm going back to the store to get some hot water."

Don't move? I thought. Where am I going?

A short time later, the man returned. "I hope it isn't too hot," he said, "I don't want to scald you." He took some time to look things over, and then he said, "I think what I'll do is heat up the railing around you. Maybe that will free you without my having to pour it on the spot where your tongue is." I carefully twisted my head and rolled my eyes until I was able to see part of the pail as he held it about a foot from my face, and then I watched in silence as the hot water spilled onto the railing. Steam rose as he moved the pail closer, and just as I felt his hand touch my face, my tongue came free. I jumped off the cement footing and back onto the sidewalk.

"Are you OK?" the man asked.

I nodded yes as I moved my tongue back and forth in my mouth to see if anything was missing. The part that had been against the metal felt tingly and it chilled the roof of my mouth, but other than that, everything seemed to be working fine. "Did any of my tongue come off?" I asked, sticking it out.

"You lost some skin and the tongue might sting for a while, but it should heal quickly," the man said.

I thanked him, and Jean and I headed back to the Children's Home. I didn't tell anyone about what happened, and evidently no one from church had called to see why we didn't show up, so the matter never came up for discussion. Unfortunately, however, it wouldn't be the last mishap I would have while I lived in the orphanage. But at least that wouldn't happen until the end of the year, so there would yet be more fun and games.

CHAPTER 34
Olli, Olli, Oxen Free

I have never felt completely comfortable within organized groups. I make friends easily enough, but I'm not crazy about the collective mind-set. Thus I have never been known to run with a pack for any length of time, whereas my sister always seemed to end up at or near the top of the popularity list of any group she belonged too. Translated, I was an outsider at the Children's Home, while she was an insider and thus forever getting privileges. I scraped for every ounce of respect I got, and my privileges were rare. But that pursuit did lead down an exciting and, at times, constructive path. I say "at times" because there has always been a destructive side to this character trait.

The path I speak of is sports. My first memories of competing successfully in physical contests came while I was in the orphanage, and with so many children to play with, there was never a shortage of competitive games.

The journey began when I learned to ride a bike. The actual

sports conquests would come later, but learning to ride opened doors otherwise closed to me. It all started when I noticed five or six of the older boys taking turns riding up and down the block on the Home's one and only bike. I envied them, and I longed for an opportunity to take my own turn, but I had two problems: first, there was only one bike, and second, I didn't know how to ride. I needed someone to teach me and I needed time to learn. An answer began to form when one of the boys jokingly told me that he would teach me to ride the bike if I gave him some candy. I didn't have any candy at the time, but a solution presented itself the following weekend. On our way back to the Home from a visit to Aunt Irene's, Mom made her usual stop at the convenience store to let us pick out treats. As I stood in the candy aisle looking at all of the choices, my eyes lit upon a bag of bubble gum. It was fat and filled with dozens of individually wrapped pieces. I hesitated, thinking about the cigarette candy and how good it would taste, and then I picked the bag up and showed it to Mom. "Can I have this?" I begged.

"Terry, that's too much," she replied. "You can't eat all that by yourself. Your teeth will fall out."

"It's not for me," I said. "I'm not going to eat *any* of it. I'm going to give some of it to a boy at the Home. He said he would teach me how to ride the bike if I gave him candy. I'll use the rest to get extra turns on the bike." I begged and pleaded until Mom finally gave in.

It took only one morning. The balancing part came easily, but the stopping took longer. For some reason, I couldn't get the hang of pushing backwards on the pedals, so at first, whenever I wanted to stop, I would intentionally head for the curb. When the front tire hit, I would go flying into, and sometimes over, the handlebars. I still didn't have the hang of it when we stopped for dinner, but during the meal something inside me clicked, and when I returned to biking in the afternoon, I rode up and down the street like a champ. The gum bought me all the time I needed.

Once I joined the bike crowd, my status at the Children's Home changed. The older boys invited me to join them on the playground across the street from the Home, and from there I graduated to Chester Creek. The playground swings and teeter-totters provided by the city were still attractive and bigger than the ones owned by the orphanage, but it was Chester Creek that got my full attention. Maybe it was the unenforced rule about not going there that made it so enticing, or maybe it was just the danger. Whatever the reason, I eagerly joined the older boys, and we spent hours horsing around on the rocks and in the creek. We would dangle our feet in the rushing water or cool off in one of the small pools carved out of the rock. The footing was slippery. One misstep on the smooth rock and we could easily break a wrist or, worse yet, split open our heads.

The waterfall at the base of the Fourth Street Bridge was the most dangerous section of the creek. There, the drop is steep and the rocks jagged, especially in the center. Despite this, in the spring, when the rushing water is at its peak, we would slide down the smooth rocks at one side of the falls and plunge into the pool, undeterred by tales of a neighborhood boy who had drowned there.

We didn't have organized sports like baseball or basketball with coaches and umpires, but we did organize our own games, and we set the rules. Olli, Olli, Oxen Free; hide and seek; Anti, Anti, I Over (Annie, Annie Over to some); and jacks were the games I excelled at, and with thirty-five to forty participants, they were always challenging. My early successes in these games not only lifted my confidence but also went a long way toward improving my standing in the pecking order.

Of all the games, Olli, Olli, Oxen Free was probably my favorite. I didn't know it at the time, but we were putting a different twist on the game. We combined Olli, Olli, Oxen Free with hide and seek and tag. The idea was to run and hide and then sneak back to the front steps of the Home and yell, "Olli, Olli, Oxen Free." If the designated "It" person tagged you before reaching the front steps, you would join him or her in the hunt for the rest of the players. Sometimes we had as many as fifteen or twenty children looking for one child.

It didn't take me long to realize that my best chance of making it to the front steps at the beginning of a game was to stay close to the Home and wait until some of the younger children made a dash for the front steps. Then I would follow, using the confusion and my quickness to evade the tag. As the game progressed and the number of "It" children increased, I would move further away from the Home. Often I would hide down by the creek, venturing out only when I saw the kids disperse in different directions or sometimes even give up. Once I waited until it was dark. When I finally got to the steps and yelled "Olli, Olli, Oxen Free," there was no one there to greet me. They were all inside getting ready for bed.

During the winter months, the outside games were not competitive, but they were fun. The Children's Home provided a few sleds, and a toboggan that held up to ten children at a time, but this wasn't enough for everyone, so we took turns. The toboggan run started at the edge of the playground. It went diagonally down the steep embankment of Chester Creek, across a flat area, and onto the ice. The trick to going the full distance was to put your feet in the lap of the girl or boy in front to eliminate drag. Anyone caught dragging his or her feet in the snow got an earful afterwards. Usually, one of the older boys would sit third from the front and steer with the pull rope. Years later, I tried this with other toboggans, but it never worked as efficiently as the toboggan at the orphanage.

Besides sledding, we skated. The city flooded one end of the playground during the winter, and they kept the warming shack open in the evenings and on weekends. I learned to skate with dual runners that strapped onto my black leather boots. I can still hear their clap against the ice as I made one failed attempt after another to glide across. When I got older, the Home gave me a pair of used figure skates. Besides being too big, they weren't stiff enough to support my ankles, so I spent more time walking on the sides than I did gliding on the blades. What I really wanted was a pair of skates like those worn by the Williams brothers, who spent hours at the rink. Sometimes I watched them as they practiced in the hockey rink next to the open ice, and at night as I lay in bed, I listened to their sticks as they connected with the rubber puck. I dreamed of one day chasing the puck across the ice on my own pair of hockey skates.

During a winter blizzard or a summer storm, the games and activities moved indoors to the dungeon. Actually, it was the basement, but we called it the dungeon because the rooms were dark and dirty, with narrow hallways that twisted and turned in no particular direction. There were no easily identifiable exit doors, and some of the passageways came to dead ends, while others went in circles. It was like finding your way through a labyrinth. Some of the older boys hinted that bodies of dead orphans were behind the locked doors. In addition to its scary and dismal appearance, the basement was always either damp or freezing, depending on the time of year. During the summer, my clothes would cling to my body, and afterwards they smelled like mold. In the winter the tiled floor stuck to my skin. If I stood in one place for too long my legs would start to ache as the coldness made its way into my bones. Sitting on the floor was even worse because after a while it numbed my butt, so I had to keep shifting positions to stay comfortable.

The playroom in the basement could accommodate most, if not all, of the children at one time. We played organized games like Ring-Around-The-Rosy, Simon Says, Musical Chairs, and of course Mrs. Scheidler's favorite game—square dancing. If no one from staff was on hand to run an activity, we would keep ourselves busy in small groups. The younger children played with kiddie toys at one end of the room, while the older girls played with dolls and the older boys with jacks and marbles. Marbles wasn't my game, but with my exceptional quickness and excellent hand-eye coordination, I excelled at jacks. In fact, it didn't take long before the boys at the orphanage refused to play with me and I had to take my talents on the road—the school playground.

The year after I arrived, a benefactor donated an electric air hockey table, and for a time it was at one end of the playroom. I quickly became addicted to the game, and then one day the table just disappeared. A boy later told me that Mr. Kolander put it in his room because some boys were squabbling over it. I think he did it so the staff could enjoy the game in private.

When summer rolled around again, my activities moved in a somewhat different direction. I would often get out early and take the bike to a neighboring alley where I played with some boys from school until it was time for dinner. Upon my return, I would put the bike into the shed, and if no one found out, I would repeat this little deception in the afternoon. This worked for a while, but eventually Mr. Kolander got wind of what I was doing and took my bike privileges away for a full month. I never went back to riding after the privileges were restored. The bike was getting too small, and I had lost interest.

After that, I joined some of the older boys for jaunts to the bar district. We would take a handful of brown paper bags from the kitchen and pick up cigarette butts from the gutters as we made our way downtown. There, we sold them to bums for a penny a dozen. A penny was worth something in those days. You could get hard candy from the jar on the counter for a penny, or you could buy a Baby Ruth bar or a pack of gum for five cents. On the way back to the orphanage, we would stop at a corner store and spend everything we made. I don't remember any malicious behavior or vandalism by any of my fellow orphans, but almost everything we did that summer was against the rules. If I was in the mood, I played Olli, Olli, Oxen Free, but by this time, some of the children had begun taking exception to my presence.

[I'd like to say it was because I was too fast and agile for most of them, and to a certain extent that was true, but unfortunately there was a destructive side to my competitive nature. I don't know if I was born this way or if it started in the orphanage, but over the years I've gotten angry at myself during sporting events and I've driven myself to extremes, sometimes to the point of complete exhaustion. For instance, towards the end of a wrestling match in high school, the coach revived me with smelling salts between the second and third overtime, and I went on to win the championship. However, I paid a price. I went blind for an hour after the event and I ended up in bed for a week, unable to move. A doctor later told me that I had most likely damaged my autoimmune system. As an adult, I suffered a heart attack during a tennis match, but I played out the final two games to win. I was back playing within a month, and I still play tennis three to four times a week. Getting angry at myself during a game, however, was the real problem. It's a form of self-abasement, and I think that's why the children at the orphanage got to the point where they didn't want to play with me anymore. Instead of giving them credit for making a good play (catching me), I would get angry and verbally abuse myself. Fortunately, with age and maturity, I've learned to control this anger. I still push myself, but I seldom get angry anymore. When I do, I try to remember to look at my opponent and say, "Nice play." This takes the sting out and it gets me refocused.]

CHAPTER 35
The Entertainment

I never had time to reflect on the past in the Home or, for that matter, to ponder the future. Each day brought a new adventure—new opportunities and options were abundant. If someone wanted to start a game, all they had to do was walk around yelling, "Let's play such and such," and within minutes, an army of children would gather, eager and ready to go.

Besides sports, the Home offered other entertainment. Once a year, we walked single file up the street to Chester Bowl for the annual picnic, and on Decoration Day (now called Memorial Day) we walked downtown to watch the parade. During one such parade, I don't remember which year it was, a stranger holding his daughter on his shoulder asked her, "See that man sitting in the car?"

"Yes!" she replied from her lofty perch.

"That's Albert Woolson, the last living veteran of the Grand Old Army of the North. Remember this moment, because when you're my age you'll be able to tell your children that you saw the last living Union soldier from the Civil War."

I pushed my way past some onlookers to get a better look, and sure enough, an elderly man was sitting in a convertible waving feebly at the crowd. He was wearing a blue uniform with a funny-looking flat-top cap. That event would have faded from my memory if it hadn't been for that complete stranger and my desire to be a witness to that moment in history.

Some of the children at the Home went to the YMCA. The Y had an indoor swimming pool and a basketball court. Because seating space in the Home's one and only vehicle was limited, only a select few were invited. Who did the selecting and what standards were used to decide who went and who didn't is unknown to me. I just know that I seldom went. One event that I did attend is memorable. It involved the Duluth Dukes, a semi-pro baseball team. The Dukes had invited all of the older boys at the orphanage to attend a basketball clinic, and I got to ride in a school bus for the first time. No one ever explained to me why a professional baseball team put on a basketball clinic, but since I didn't know what a baseball team was, it wouldn't have mattered one way or the other. I had seen kids playing ball at school and at the playground across the street from the orphanage, but I had never seen a real baseball game. The clinic frustrated me. Because of my short stature, I had a difficult time dribbling the ball, and when I did get a chance to shoot, the ball barely cleared the heads of the other boys, let alone making it to the basket. At the start of the clinic, we all received a T-shirt with "Duluth Dukes" across the front. [I still have that T-shirt, and each of my daughters wore it when they were toddlers.]

The Children's Home did not have a radio or a television set, but they did provide live performances. Once a month a new entertainer would come to the Home and put on a show. This included piano recitals, singers, clowns, ventriloquists, storytellers, and magicians. I could sit for hours listening to a good storyteller, but I walked out on bad ones, and I didn't bother with piano recitals. It was a magician who made a lasting impression. The rabbit in the hat and the card tricks were fun to watch, but I completely lost it when he cut his hand off in the guillotine, and I wasn't alone. Everyone in the audience let out a gasp, and after several children ran out of the room screaming, one of the matrons said, "I think you went too far with that one." Realizing his mistake, he showed us his hand and said, "It's just a trick. See, I'm OK, I didn't really cut it off."

After the show, the magician invited anyone who had an interest in learning how the guillotine worked to the front of the room. He explained the illusion and how he could turn the contraption on and off. When he did the trick a second time, his hand came out attached to his arm. I was transfixed throughout the demonstration, and afterwards I asked lots of questions. Seeing my interest, he asked me if I would like to put my hand in the opening. "No!" I said as I quickly pulled my hands off the table and shoved them into my pocket. I understood how he created the illusion, but I still didn't trust him.

Saturday night was movie night, but the attendance was unpredictable. Some, like me, couldn't sit in one spot for thirty minutes, while others, again like me, couldn't read the schedule posted on the entertainment door. If and when I did watch a show, it was usually after someone told me that a Laurel and Hardy or an *Our Gang* movie was showing and then only if I wasn't involved in something more active.

After the departure of Mrs. Scheidler, the staff started treating us to an occasional movie in one of the theaters downtown, but this was rare and used as a reward for good behavior. I didn't get invited to go until shortly after my seventh birthday in 1952. The movie showing that day was *The Greatest Show on Earth*, and it would turn out be the beginning of a climactic series of traumatic events.

CHAPTER 36
The Greatest Show on Earth

Not long after my seventh birthday, Mr. Kolander drove me and several other children from the orphanage to one of the downtown theaters to see a movie called *The Greatest Show on Earth*. He said it was my birthday gift, but I think it was more a reward for good behavior, or maybe it was a little of both. He didn't stay for the movie, but before he left, he gave us a lecture about keeping quiet, and then he told us to wait for him in the lobby when the movie was over.

This was the first time I had ever been inside a theater. I had watched television through the window of a store once, and I had watched short black-and-white reels in the entertainment room at the Home, but this show was a whole two hours long and in living Technicolor. We arrived a half-hour before show time. Some of the kids sat at the back while others ran to the front, but because it was an early matinee, the theater stayed empty, so by the time the show started most of us had gathered in the middle. The movie was about a circus troupe that traveled around the country, and I quickly got caught up in the drama. About a third of the way through the movie, one of the boys sitting close to me whispered, "Terry, your name is on the screen."

Caught off guard, I said, "What?"

"Your name is on the bottom of the screen! See?"

My eyes shifted from the scene of a lion's cage to where he was pointing, but I didn't see anything other than what was in the movie.

"It said for you to go to the front," one of the older girls whispered from the next row.

"Up in front by the screen?" I whispered, agitated because I hadn't seen my name and confused by what the children were saying. Maybe the boy was just playing a joke on me, but the girl wouldn't do that; I hardly knew her.

"No, silly, where we came in!"

Reluctantly, I got up, skirted the knees of the boy next to me, and walked to the back of the theater. An attendant opened the swinging doors and I stepped into the lobby. It took a few seconds for my eyes to adjust to the bright lights, but when they did, I saw my mom and my sister and brother standing just inside the front entrance. Next to them stood a man who looked somewhat familiar.

"Terry, do you know who this is?" my mother asked.

"No."

"This is your father, and he's come back to live with us! We're going to be a *real family* again. Isn't that wonderful?"

I didn't know what to do or say. I didn't rush to him, and I didn't get excited or rattled. I was skeptical and afraid. He had come back before, and it had never turned out the way our mother expected it to.

His physical appearance hadn't changed that much. He still wore the same brown tinted glasses, his hair was cut short, sweat glistened off the top of his deeply tanned forehead, shirt sleeves folded up to his elbows exposed bulging muscles, and his tattoo still showed through the thick hair on his arms.

"Are you glad to see me?" he asked, as if I had been waiting impatiently for his return. "You've grown into quite the young man since I saw you last." Bending over, he extended his right hand to me. I put my hand in his and felt the firmness of his grip as he said, "You remember your old man, don't you?"

I shook my head yes, but I didn't smile.

"Well, we're going to get to know each other better because I'm back for good. Here, do you like candy?" he asked, holding out a Snickers bar.

"Yes," I said, taking the bar.

"Good. That's good," he said, patting me on the back. He turned and opened the glass door, expecting me to follow.

"Mom, I want to watch the rest of the show," I said, not moving.

"Your dad's taking us to the Honkalas to celebrate. You remember Alfred and Martha Honkala, don't you?"

"We can go there afterwards," I said, not bothering to answer her question.

"Come on!" I heard my father say impatiently to no one in particular. "Let's go! Alfred and Martha are expecting us, and we don't want to keep them waiting."

"He's not my boss," I snarled at my mother as I walked past her into the sunlight. I was also walking into something else—something that would become one of the most painful deceptions a man can inflict on a woman.

CHAPTER 37
The Reunion

Duluth, Minnesota, September 1952. From the theater, we drove through town, and fifteen minutes later our dad pulled up in front of a two-story wood-frame building that, with its flat roofline, looked like it might have been a general store at one time. "Well, here we are," he said. "This is where Alfred and Martha live."

We entered the building through a side door and climbed a set of steep narrow stairs. Looking up, I saw, not a door or entryway, but rather the high ceiling of what appeared to be the second floor. When I reached the top step, I was surprised to see that we were standing in one huge room that extended from one end of the building to the other. The only light in the room came from two windows that faced the street and from somewhere at the back. Despite this, it was dark and gloomy in the room and smoke hung in the air. I could smell cigarette smoke, but there was a hint of something else—probably bacon from breakfast, I thought, or just stale air.

Household furnishings scattered throughout acted as the partitioning walls. The living room was in the center. There, two bulky sofas, one with a sheet thrown over it, defined the length of the living room, and between the sofas stood a rather plain-looking, beat-up coffee table. Two matching armchairs with threadbare armrests and end tables defined the living room's width.

A large open space between the living room and windows was bare of furniture. Linoleum covered the wooden floor of the space to within a yard of the outside walls. There, old trunks, cardboard boxes, piles of magazines, and other miscellaneous junk littered the floor.

What must have at one time been an elegant dining set was on the opposite side of the living room—directly behind one of the sofas. I say "elegant" because the dark-stained, shiny tabletop was thin and decorative, not bulky like other tables I had seen, and the matching chairs were decorative and delicate. To the left of the table and directly in front of where we stood sat a white porcelain stove, and standing in front of it was a short, plump woman in a print dress and apron. I could tell she had been baking because there was flour on her hands and her face was red and sweaty. Sweeping her curly dishwater blond hair away from her face, she put down the spoon she was holding and rushed toward us. "Well, hi! Is this your family, Nels?"

"Martha, do you remember Eileen?" Dad asked.

"Hi, Eileen, it's good to see you again, and hi, kids," Martha said, bending over and getting into our faces. "You remember me, don't you, Terry? You must have been, what…"

"Terry was four when you saw him the last time," said Mom.

"Oh, that *is* a long time ago. Four, and you're how old now?"

"Seven," I muttered, almost incoherently.

"Seven! My, you've grown so big."

I suddenly remembered that time, long ago, when I had taken my sister and brother into the bar to get our dad.

"And Larry, you've grown so big too," Martha continued. "You were a baby the last time I saw you, and Jean, you're quite the young lady. My, my, you've grown. I have a daughter your age. I'm sure the two of you will have lots of fun, won't you?"

By this time her two daughters were standing next to her. The smaller one was still in diapers. All I really remember about them is that the older daughter wore glasses with pop bottle lenses and she had the most amazing hair. If ever there was a head of hair that belonged in the story of *Goldilocks and the Three Bears*, it was hers. Thick golden ringlets hung down to her shoulders, and her bangs curled into perfect little circles.

"Alfred, come and meet Nels and Eileen's children!" Martha screamed in my ear. "Do you remember them?" Martha's husband, who had been sitting on one of the sofas, attempted to get up, but he was either drunk or had vertigo because he fell back onto the sofa's cushion, nearly spilling the drink he held in his hand. Grabbing the armrest with his free hand, he made a second attempt, and with some effort, he managed to pull himself to a standing position.

"Hey, kids, want a beer?" Alfred asked, almost tipping over one of the lamps. The adults must have thought his comment was funny, because they laughed. "Nels, I bet you want something to drink if the kids don't. What'll you have, something hard, or a beer?"

"I'll have what you're having, Alfred," Dad said.

"There you go, bring him a whiskey *and* a beer, Martha," he demanded.

"Would you like something to drink, Eileen?" Martha asked.

"I'll just have some of that coffee. Maybe I'll have a drink later," Mom replied.

"Don't pay any attention to my husband, kids," Martha said, looking at our mother and shrugging, "he's already drunk. Aren't you, Alfred?"

"Thass right, I'm already drunk. Thass the only way to be... isn't that right, Nels?"

"Right, Alfred!"

Alfred was skinny and maybe six inches taller than my father, which wasn't saying much. Like Martha's, his voice was raspy from smoking too much, but unlike hers, it was loud and foul. After Martha brought my dad a drink, he and Alfred retired to the living room. Mom and Martha stood next to the stove talking while Larry and Jean and the two Honkala girls went off to play in the open area behind the sofa. With no one my age to play with, I moved into the living room. I sat down in one of the armchairs, tucked my hands under my legs, and listened as the men bragged about this or that with a swagger and bravado that nauseated me. The family reunion had turned into a farce.

Every so often, Alfred would get up to go to the bathroom, giving my dad and me an opportunity to talk. It didn't amount to much. How are things at the orphanage? Are you learning much in school? Things like that. During one of Alfred's trips, he must have tried to steady himself on a dining room chair, because I heard him and the chair crash to the floor with a thud and Martha saying, "Alfred, are you all right?"

"I'm fine, woman. That damned chair got in my way. What the hell did you put it in the middle of the aisle for?"

I watched him as he stumbled from the kitchen into another area behind the stove and then down a hallway and out of sight. It was then that I noticed a small kitchen table that sat against a wall in the area behind the stove. This, I guessed, must be where the family ate most of their meals. The wall was maybe seven feet high or about halfway to the ceiling. It extended from one side of the main room to the other with a hallway down its center. This must be where they slept, I thought. Behind the dining room table, I spotted a ladder that extended straight up to an open loft above the wall. The space in the loft was crammed full of boxes and junk, including an old chair with a hole in the seat.

"Terry," Martha said, interrupting my reveries, "if you climb up that ladder you'll find some toys that used to belong to our boys. I didn't know what she meant by "our boys," but she didn't have to ask me twice.

I ran behind the dining room table and quickly climbed the ladder. When I got to the top, I stepped onto the floor-boards and looked around, searching for toys, but seeing none, I moved back to the ladder and yelled, "I don't see any toys up here."

"Are you sure?"

"Yes. There's just boxes and stuff."

"Alfred, what did you do with the boys' toys?" Martha shouted.

"Toys? What are you talking about, woman, and what's he doing up there?" Alfred said as he returned from the bathroom. "There's nothing up there for him."

"I thought he could play with some of the things that be-longed to the boys."

"I got rid of all those old toys," he said, "and I don't want him going though all that stuff. Get him down from there."

"I'm sorry, Terry. I guess you'll have to play with whatever you can find," Martha said as I carefully climbed back down.

With no one to play with and nothing to do, I wandered down the hallway, poking my head into each of the rooms. The girls' bedroom was the first one on the left, behind the kitchen. I poked my head in and saw my sister and the two Honkala girls playing with their dolls. They ignored me, so I left and walked to the next door. Opening it, I peered inside. An old-fashioned bathtub with spindly legs stood against the wall to my left; directly in front of me was the washbasin and beyond that the toilet. Not needing to go, I backed out and walked to the far end of the hall. Putting the palms of my hands against the back door and standing on my tiptoes, I peered through the window that took up the upper half of the door. In front of me, I saw the top of a wood railing that I reasoned must be the fire escape, and far below that a large yard that bordered the backs of other homes. I couldn't see any swings or slides, but I thought there might be something to play with between the houses, so I yelled, "Can I go down the fire escape?"

I heard who I think was Martha, shouting, "No, that fire escape isn't safe. You stay inside."

Then I heard someone else say, "What did he say?"

"He asked if he could do down the fire escape and I told him no."

With that option closed, I walked over to the door on the opposite side of the hallway and opened it. The door led into what I thought must be the master bedroom. The room was clean and sparsely furnished. An adult-sized bed took up most of the space. The only other objects were a stand-up dresser, a nightstand, and a chair that sat next to the bed. Double doors on the wall to my left most likely opened to a closet.

Having seen everything and bored stiff, I walked back to the living room and sat down next to my mother. The adults were talking and arguing about things that didn't make a lot of sense to me, but shortly after my return, my father boasted about how grown up I had become, and my mother said something about me being her "little man." This at least gave me a sense of being included in the conversation.

In the middle of all the talk, one of the adults asked me to get the coffee pot. I also seem to recall another voice saying, "I don't think he's big enough to reach up that far." I know for sure that I ran to the stove and, without thinking, reached for the handle of the coffee pot. As I did so, I heard my mother say, "Here, Terry let me help you, it's hot!" She was too late. I felt a searing sensation as the flesh on my hand melted against the hot metal. I pulled my hand away, bringing the pot of hot coffee down on top of me. Fortunately, it missed my face, but it soaked the front of my shirt, and when it hit the floor I felt it splash onto my legs.

I clutched at my shirt in an attempt to tear the burning sensation away from me, screaming at the top of my lungs. Someone carried me into the bathroom and took my clothes off. Then I heard someone say, "Put him in the tub and run the cold water and I'll bring some ice." I remember the floating ice cubes, the rattling of my teeth, and the water rippling from the shaking of my body. When my mother finally decided I'd been in the water long enough, she lifted me out and, with encouragement from Martha and my father, rubbed butter on the fresh wounds that had already started to form blisters. I was still shaking from the cold water as Mom brought me into the master bedroom and put me under the covers to get warm.

The ice had done its job, because after only a short time I felt a lot better and I asked my mother if I could get out of bed.

She told me that my father had gone out to buy new clothes and that as soon as he returned I could get up. Within the hour, he was back with a new shirt and pants. I dressed, and then my father asked me to do something that was totally out of character for him: he asked me if I'd like to go for a walk. I say "out of character" because I don't remember ever spending time alone with him, and he had never spoken to me in confidence. His words didn't particularly suggest intimacy, but their intonation did, so I willingly went with him. The adults, including my mother, didn't say a thing as we passed them on our way to the staircase, a sure sign (in retrospect) that the unfolding event had been agreed to ahead of time.

"You had a close call, young man. You could have been hurt a lot worse. Do you feel better?" he asked as we walked down a sharp grade.

"Yes," I mumbled.

"Good, that's my boy. You're as tough as your old man, aren't you?"

I didn't say anything. I had heard those words before and they didn't do a thing for me. Then something caught my attention—a man in his mid-twenties walking towards us. His clothes were ordinary enough—jeans, high-top riding boots, and a tight black pullover shirt. What struck me as odd was his left leg. It was facing in the opposite direction. I don't mean slanted or pigeon-toed, but backwards, as in one hundred and eighty degrees. He didn't drag the leg like someone with an injury but instead lifted it and flung it forward in a kind of arching motion. As he did this, he gave a little hop with his left leg. It looked awkward.

"How come that man's leg is on backwards?" I asked.

"He was born that way, and don't point. That's not nice."

"I'm not pointing," I said, dropping my arm.

My father must have known the man because he yelled, "Hi, Stan!" Then he said something in a language that I didn't understand and the man responded in kind. When I asked my mom later why he talked so funny, she told me they were speaking in Finnish. They shouted back and forth in that foreign way, and then Dad said in English, "Terry, say hi to Stan."

I mumbled hi, and my father and the man continued to talk as he hopped away.

After the man was out of earshot, my father bent down on one knee, looked me straight in the eye, and said, "I need to ask you to do something. Can you do something for me?"

I nodded, but I didn't know what he had in mind.

"Do you think you can keep this accident to yourself? I mean, when we take you back to the orphanage, do you think you can keep quiet about what happened?"

"I thought Mom said we weren't going back."

He paused for a second and then said, "I don't have a place for us to live right now, so we'll have to bring you back to the Children's Home for the time being. It won't be for long, but if you tell them about the accident they might not let your mother see you again. You don't want that, do you?"

I shook my head no. I should have picked up on something from his comment about my mother, but I didn't.

"Good, then we have an agreement. You might have to keep your shirt on until the wounds heal. You can do that, can't you?"

"I think so," I said, not completely understanding what he meant by keeping my shirt on. Did he mean I couldn't change it? What would I do when it got dirty?

Then he reached into his pocket and brought something

out. "This is for you. I don't want you to tell your brother and sister about it, because I didn't get them a present, so it's our little secret. Can you keep a secret?"

"Yes!" I said, excited by what I saw in his hand.

"Have you ever seen a knife like this? It's a replica of a real Jim Bowie knife."

I didn't know what he meant by Jim Bowie, but when he pulled it out of its leather sheath and held it out to me, I could see that it was unlike any knife I had ever seen before. The handle was ivory and the blade shiny and curved, with a serrated edge on the dull side. I took it in my hand and felt the edge of the blade. The knife was sharp and surprisingly heavy for its three-inch size.

"Is it really mine?" I asked.

"Yes, but you have to remember not to tell anyone at the orphanage about the accident. Can you do that?" I nodded. "And you'll have to hide the knife, because if they find it they'll take it away." Again, I nodded. I slipped the knife into my pocket, and we walked back to the house.

I never did tell anyone at the orphanage about the accident. I would sneak butter from the dining room table and afterwards go to my room and smear it on the burns, which left stains on my shirts. Since I had the room to myself, changing shirts was never a problem. Because the burns were ugly and obvious, I didn't take a bath with the other kids. Instead, I washed myself by hand. After a couple of weeks, the dead skin tissue went away and things returned to normal. As for the knife, I hid it in my room. At Christmas, it would prove to come in handy, and later it would be instrumental in bringing my mother and me back together.

The last photo of Lillian Larson with her grandchildren taken somewhere in Duluth, Minnesota in 1952. From Left to right: Larry, Jean, Lillian, and Terry

CHAPTER 38

An Angel on High

After our parents returned us to the orphanage, we never saw or heard from them. It was as if they had fallen off the face of the earth. Our mother's visits had become erratic after our last visit to the farm during the summer of 1951, but to not hear from her at all was puzzling. Uncle Alan and Grandma did drop by once, out of the blue. They took us out of the Home for the afternoon. An estimate based on a photo would place the visit most likely during the spring of 1952.

Fall quickly turned into winter that year. The Christmas season was upon us and it was time to trim the big tree. Each year a Christmas tree would be brought in and placed in the lobby under the chandelier, which the maintenance man would move aside by tying it to the ceiling. Only the older children got to take part in the trimming, and at least one staff member was always present. Because I had turned seven that past summer and for the most part had stayed out of trouble, Mr. Kolander invited me to participate, along with three other children.

Someone had strung the lights the day before, so the only thing left were the decorations. Mr. Kolander and another staffer started somewhere around the middle and worked upward, while we concentrated on the bottom half. The tree was a good twelve feet high, so when the adults were within a few feet of the top, they brought out a ladder to complete the job. When they finished, we all stood back and looked in wonder at our creation. It was beautiful, especially the tinsel which hung in gobs from every branch. The only piece missing was the angel.

"Would someone like the honor of putting the angel on the top branch?" Mr. Kolander asked.

"I will, I will!" we all shouted in unison as we pushed and shoved each other to get our hands on the coveted decoration.

"OK, let's see, how can we choose, since you all want to do it? How about eeny, meeny, miny, mo?" Mr. Kolander patted each of us on the head as he recited the nursery rhyme, ending up with, you guessed it, me. "Do you think you're big enough to reach the top branch from the ladder, Terry?" he asked, somewhat reluctantly.

I nodded, grabbed the angel out of his hand, and almost ran up the ladder. When I got to the second step from the top, I reached out to place the angel, only to find that I was a good foot too low.

"I think you'll have to go to the next step," Mr. Kolander said from somewhere below me. "Do you want me to do it?"

"No, I can do it!" I said enthusiastically. Clinging to the top rung, I climbed to the next step. Reaching out with my right hand and holding on for dear life with my left, I stretched as far as I could. To my disappointment, the tip of the branch was still a few inches away. With my right arm still extended, I slid my left hand to the edge of the ladder and wrapped two of my fingers around one of the boards holding the top platform. On my tiptoes and with the weight of my torso on those two fingers, I tried one last time, knowing that if this didn't work, I would have to give up. Just as I was about to drop the angel into place, the ladder started to shake violently, as if someone had bumped it or was intentionally shaking it. Instinctively, I pulled myself back, but my fingers slipped, and I went head first into the tree.

I must have hit every branch on the way down, because I ended up with scratches all over my face and bruises everywhere. Fortunately, Mr. Kolander had grabbed the tree before it crashed on top of me, but that didn't stop the decorations from flying all over the place.

Despite my miraculous deliverance, I caught hell from all directions. The children yelled at me for destroying their Christmas tree, and Mr. Kolander scolded me for not listening to him. If I had had my wits about me, I would have yelled at him for not holding the ladder steady, but I didn't think of it at the time, and when I did it was too late to say anything. Besides, it might have been one or more of the boys who were holding it.

Mr. Kolander righted the tree, and for the rest of the afternoon the children went about the redecorating while I watched from the triangle behind the glass entrance door, pulling needles out of my hair and clothes.

CHAPTER 39

My Very Own Christmas Tree

I could never understand why Mr. Kolander disciplined me for what, in my view, was an accident and, if anything, more his fault than mine. In retaliation, I refused to have anything to do with the Christmas tree in the lobby. I pouted and said some nasty things about how it looked, and I went out of my way to ignore it, but no one paid any attention.

Shortly after the incident, I came up with my own idea for a Christmas tree. While sitting on my bedroom window ledge one afternoon, I spotted a perfect little evergreen growing in the front yard of a neighboring house. Wouldn't it be wonderful, I thought, if it was sitting in my room? It was the perfect size, and with a few decorations, I would have my very own Christmas tree! I didn't need that stupid old tree downstairs, and it would serve them right for what they had done to me.

It took me almost a full week to cut the tree down. I would sneak out of the Home after dark, run to the neighbor's front yard and, lying on my stomach, whittle at the trunk with my little three-inch Jim Bowie knife until my arms got tired. Fortunately, the neighbors didn't look out their front window during the day, because if they had, they would have seen footprints on the frozen ground and the imprint of a small body at the base of the tree. On the fourth day, the tree began to lean. Knowing that I couldn't finish before bedtime, I propped it up with sticks. On the evening of the fifth day, the trunk finally yielded.

I hauled the tree into the Home and up three flights of stairs without anyone seeing me. Once I was in my room, I stuck the tree into a rotted old log that I had found several days earlier. Then I trimmed it with a string of popcorn and rings of colored paper taped together to form a long chain. I didn't have lights or an angel and it leaned a little to the left, but I was the only boy in the Children's Home to have his very own Christmas tree.

My pride of ownership didn't last long. The next day Mr. Kolander walked into my room and asked, "Where did that come from?" Without hesitation, I walked over to the window and proudly pointed at the neighbor's yard.

"From over there."

"Over there?" he asked, nodding in the general direction of the neighbor's house.

"Yup," I said. "I cut it down and made all of the decorations by myself."

"How did you cut it down?"

I pulled the knife out of my pocket and showed it to him.

"With that little thing?" he asked, taking the knife out of my hand and putting it into his pocket. "It must have taken you most of the week."

"What are you going to do with my knife?"

"I'm going to give it to Mrs. Hemphill, but before I do, you and I are going over to the neighbor's house to apologize."

I went willingly, but for some reason Mr. Kolander felt that it was necessary to hold onto my right ear. When the neighbor appeared at the door, Mr. Kolander said, "This young man has something to tell you."

I told the man everything, leaving out no details. I even told him the story about my grandpa cutting down the neighbor's Christmas tree. After I finished, he shook his head and laughed. Then he said, "That's quite a story, young man. I guess I should be mad at you, but to be honest, I didn't even notice the tree was missing." Still laughing, he said, "Besides, I think you did it for the right reasons, so I'll let it pass this time, but you can't go around cutting people's trees down. You might get by with it on your grandpa's farm, but not in town."

So I apologized, and after he and Mr. Kolander talked for a bit, we left. But I didn't forget about my knife.

CHAPTER 40
An Orphan's Christmas

I never looked forward to Christmases at the orphanage. The cooks would prepare a big feast on Christmas day, and community contributors and parents were invited to dine with the children, but to me the food wasn't the same as Grandma's, and the atmosphere was never as cozy or warm. The fact that our mother never came most likely contributed to my less-than-festive feelings, but I think it's safe to say that for many of the children, Christmas at the Children's Home was what one would expect: institutional.

After the noon meal, we would be herded into the entertainment room, where we sang carols and when we ran out of songs, one of the adults would read a Christmas story. Then, around three o'clock, Santa would show up with his "Ho, ho, ho and a Merry Christmas!" and we would chorus, "Merry Christmas, Santa!" He would put his sack on the floor and pull out a brown paper bag with a name on it. "Alice or Jimmy or Tommy (whatever the name happened to be), were you good this year?" That person would always answer with a resounding YES. Then he would ask the child to come to the front, where he would hand them the proverbial bag of popcorn balls, shelled peanuts, and hard candy—the same brown paper bag we carried our lunch to school in. When everyone had their bag, he would give a final "Ho, ho, ho, and a Merry Christmas," and exit. We were then excused, ending our Christmas.

Occasionally a wealthy Duluth family would invite an orphan to spend Christmas Eve with them. I don't know how they went about choosing the lucky child, and rest assured, I was never chosen, but my sister Jean's name was called once, and she got to spend an unforgettable evening with a family. According to her, after she unwrapped her one gift, a bathrobe, as it turned out, she got to watch the family's daughter open her many gifts, including a large drawing easel.

[That's one of those experiences an orphan never forgets, but looking at the situation from another angle, what would my sister have done with a large drawing easel? Chances are the family had been told not to get her anything big or expensive. It's too bad they didn't have their daughter open most of her presents on Christmas day. I must admit that the commercial side of Christmas has never been important to me. Maybe it has something to do with the experiences I had at the Children's Home, although, except for the food, it wasn't much better at Grandma and Grandpa's. I enjoy cooking for family and friends during the holiday season, a trait that I suspect came from my grandmother. I also appreciate the spirit of Christmas—the birth of Jesus and some of the activity behind the celebration of his birth—but I remain lukewarm on the commercial side of Christmas.]

PART VI: THE FINAL QUEST

A weathered granite bench that overlooks the parking lot and Mary's Garden at the college of St. Scholastica in Duluth, Minnesota

CHAPTER 41
Good News

Duluth, Minnesota, July 1953. I didn't hear about my brother Larry's adoption until the day of his departure, and if he hadn't gone out of his way to come to the third floor to find me, I might never have known about it. I think that was the first time he had ever been up there. I had just come out of the bathroom, and he was at the far end of the hall yelling, "I've got a new mom and dad!" while waving his arms frantically to get my attention. Then he rushed down the hall toward me.

"What do you mean?" I asked as he came within earshot.

"They took me to their house on the lake and they have a dog and a horse and I got to ride the horse and everything!" he said proudly, breathing hard.

"Wait a minute. Slow down!" I said with my palms out toward him. "What are you talking about? I never heard anything about this. When did you meet them?"

"Yesterday, and I get to go home with them *today*!" he replied, putting his hands onto his knees as he gasped for breath.

I didn't know how to react to this news, and I must admit I was a little jealous. Not about the adoption, but about all the things the new mom and dad had—the lake house, the horse. I should have been concerned that Larry was being adopted without us, but that never entered my mind. I very seldom saw him, hadn't talked to him for months, and (I hate to say it) never thought about him. Jean saw him regularly and sometimes she would tell me what was going on, but it went in one ear and out the other. Now, here he was, getting adopted before Jean and me.

That was the extent of our conversation. I don't even remember saying goodbye or good luck. Larry left the Children's Home on July 9, 1953. Things moved quickly after that. A few days later, Mrs. Hemphill asked me to come into her office. "Terry," she said in a rather matter-of-fact tone, "we've found a new mom and dad for you and your sister. They will be here tomorrow to take you to the park. Would you like to meet them?"

I didn't really know what to say. I knew that my chances of adoption were getting slimmer with each passing year. I hadn't seen my mother for a long time, not since the day I pulled the coffee pot down on top of me. Before that it had been— what—six months? Any attachment I had felt for her had long since faded, and her touch, her smell, and even the way she looked were now distant memories.

"Can I have my knife back?" I asked.

"Knife? What knife are you talking about?"

"The knife you took away from me. The one my dad gave me. It had a white handle and it was little," I said, spreading my fingers three inches apart to show her.

"Oh, now I remember. You cut a tree down with it. I almost

forgot about that."

"It was a *Christmas* tree," I said defiantly.

"OK, the Christmas tree. I think I gave the knife to your mother."

"When did you give it to her?" I asked, perturbed that they hadn't let me know.

"I guess it was a week or so after Christmas. What does it matter?"

"How come you didn't let me see her?" I asked, my anger beginning to show.

"You were in school," she answered, but there was something in the way she said it that made me wonder if she was telling the truth.

"Can you ask her to bring the knife back?" I asked, not even caring if I saw my mom at that point. "It's my knife, not hers, and I want to bring it with me to my new home."

"Terry, I'm sorry, but I don't know how to get in touch with your mother."

"Where is she?" I asked, going on the offensive.

"OK, Terry. Calm down." she said. "The last I heard, she had moved and was working in the kitchens at St. Scholastica. But that's not the point, Terry. The point is I think you're too young to have a knife."

"What's saint, saint—whatever you called it?"

"St. Scholastica. It's a Catholic school for girls and it's a long, long ways from here," she said, making it sound like a far-off planet.

I wanted to ask her how to get to the school, but I sensed that she knew she had said too much already. Miss Hemphill had not been at the Home the first time I ran away. She didn't know that when I set my mind on something, I didn't let little things get in my way.

"When are we going to see our new mom and dad?" I asked, suddenly aware of the fact that I hadn't even agreed to meet them.

She smiled and said, "Well, they'll be here tomorrow, and I think you and Jean will like them. They live on a farm. You'll like that, won't you? Didn't you live on a farm before you came here?"

"Do they have horses?" I asked, thinking about what my brother Larry had told me about his new parents.

"I don't know, but when you see them you can ask. I know they have cows and pigs, and I'll bet they even have a dog." I nodded to let her know that I thought so too. Everyone who lived on a farm had a dog.

"Would you like to know their names?" she asked, rummaging through the papers on her desk. I nodded, and when she finally found the paper she was looking for, she said, "Let's see, the dad's name is Walter and the mother's name is Winifred and their last name is Degner and they live on a farm by Wendell, Minnesota. I think that's out in western Minnesota someplace."

She was obviously unsure of her geography, but it didn't matter. What mattered was that they wanted both my sister and me. She paused for my reaction, and when it didn't come, she asked, "Do you have any questions, Terry?" I shook my head no.

"Are you going to tell my sister?"

"Yes, I'll see Jean later this morning, so if you see her, please don't say anything about our conversation. OK?"

"How come?" I asked, almost laughing, because we both knew that if I saw her first, I'd tell her everything.

"Because I think it would be best coming from me. Don't you?"

I shrugged and said, "I guess so," trying to remember what Jean had told me. I knew she was doing something important that morning, but I couldn't remember what it was.

"You run along now and play," Miss Hemphill said, shooing me away.

I didn't have to look for Jean. She ran into me as I was walking out the side door, but before I could tell her about the adoption, she squealed, "I'm moving to the big girls' cottage and they showed me the house and I got to see where I would be sleeping and they even cut my hair, see!"

"It looks like someone put a bowl on top of your head," I said in disgust.

"They did!" she said, giggling. "That's how they do it. Isn't it neat?"

"You're *not moving*," I said, changing the subject.

"What do you mean? I can move if I want and you can't stop me!" she scowled, obviously not understanding me.

"You're not moving, because Miss Hemphill found us a new mom and dad!"

"Really," she replied, her excitement turning to apprehension. "When did she say that?"

"Just now. She's going to tell you later, so you have to pretend I didn't tell you. OK?" Jean looked at me questioningly, chewing on a fingernail. "You have to promise me you won't tell her. Do you *promise*?"

"I promise." There was a pause as she digested what I was telling her, and then she asked, "Do you think our new mom and dad will be nice?"

"I don't know, but I have to find Mom first," I said firmly.

"How come? She won't be our mom anymore."

"Because she has my knife and I want it back."

"Do you know where she is?"

"Miss Hemphill said she's at a saint something. It's a girls' school."

"It's just a dumb old knife. Maybe our new mom and dad won't let you keep it."

"I don't care! It's my knife and I want it!" I shouted as I walked out the door. "Remember, don't tell her I told you," and with that, I went off in search of someone who could tell me where the "saint something" was.

CHAPTER 42
Saint Something or Other

The key to finding Saint Something or Other came within minutes of leaving my sister. I spotted Mr. and Mrs. Rassmussen by the playground in the front yard. The Rassmussens had taken charge of the girls' cottage after Mr. and Mrs. Jensen left. I didn't know them very well, but they seemed nice enough, and they didn't know me well, which, given the situation, was definitely in my favor.

"Hi, Terry," Mr. Rassmussen said. "How are you?"

"Good."

"Have you been staying out of trouble?" he asked with a big smile.

"Uh-huh. Mr. Rassmussen, do you know where the girls' school is?"

"The girls' school," he repeated, rubbing his chin in thought. "I'm not sure which school you're talking about. Do you know what it's called?"

"The Saint Something or Other," I answered. "I don't know

the exact name."

"Oh, you mean St. Scholastica?" he said, rolling his eyes.

"Yes! That's it, St. Scholastica! Do you know where it's at?"

"Why, are you going to become a nun?" he laughed.

"No," I answered, not knowing what a nun was. "Someone was talking about it and I was just wondering where it was, that's all."

"Well, that's a good one. Do you know where Chester Bowl is?"

"No."

"Do you know where the ski jump is?"

"Uh-huh, that's where we have our picnics."

"Is that right? I didn't know that. I guess we haven't been here long enough," he said, patting me on the head.

"Does this road go by the school?" I asked, pointing at the road in front of the orphanage.

"Well, not exactly, but it turns into another road that goes by the road that goes into the park, if that makes sense, and Chester Bowl gets its name from the creek that flows through the park. It's the same creek as the one over there," he said, pointing across the playground.

"Is St. Scholastica in Chester Bowl?" I asked, trying to figure out what he was talking about. I didn't remember seeing a school by the ski lifts.

"No, no. In fact, I'm not sure the road that goes by Chester Bowl will even take you to the school. It might, but it's not the best way to get there."

"Really?" I said, disappointed at this turn of events. If it didn't go by the school, how was I ever going to get there?

"Well, you asked me where the school was and I was going to say St. Scholastica is somewhere behind the ski lift, but to drive there you would need to get to Kenwood Drive and that's a little more complicated to explain. Are you planning on driving there anytime soon?"

"No," I said, knowing that he was just kidding. "I'm not big enough, but I bet I could walk there."

"I don't think so. That would be quite a walk for someone with your little legs. You would have to get to the park first and then walk up the big hill by the ski lift and then go through the woods and I'm not even sure you'd come out at the school. I know it's somewhere behind the lift but where is another question. I know I wouldn't want to walk there and besides, what would you do when you got there?"

I shrugged and smiled. "I'm not going there. I was just wondering where it was, that's all."

I waved and went back into the Home. Then I watched the Rassmussens from behind the glass in the door. They talked for a few minutes and then Mr. Rassmussen drove off. Good, I thought, now all I have to do is to wait for Mrs. Rassmussen to leave and I'll will be free to leave.

CHAPTER 43
Up the Creek

It was mid-morning when Mrs. Rassmussen walked back to the girl's cottage. To eliminate any chance of her seeing me, I exited the Home by the front door and quickly crossed the street to Chester Park. To avoid detection, I headed straight to the tree line that bordered the park and followed a well-worn pathway down a steep slope to the creek. At the base of the slope, the trail split. The one going to the left followed the creek down to Lake Superior, and I knew that going right would take me up the hill towards the ski lifts and Chester Bowl.

I couldn't have picked a better day. Rays of sunlight filtered through the leaves and the rushing water drowned out all other sounds as it cascaded over rocks, forming small whirlpools. I had often played at the creek, but I had never taken the trail to Chester Bowl. The staff had warned us not to go by ourselves and never to talk to strangers. If we saw someone hanging around, we were to report them immediately. I was never sure what they meant by "hanging around," because we saw individuals, young couples, and families by the creek all the time. Sometimes they would even roll up their pants legs and wade in the water, but they didn't bother us. One of the older girls said that she once saw a stranger talking to some kids, but as far as I knew nothing ever came of it.

The narrow dirt footpath twisted around large rocks, down small ravines, and up the steep sides of the creek without much rhyme or reason except for one thing: it was uphill. Once in a while I would stop and look back to see if someone was following me, and to try to see small patches of water through the trees to make sure Lake Superior was still there. Eventually, I lost sight of the lake completely. There's something reassuring about knowing where you've been, even if you don't know where you're going.

The uphill climb was slow and I soon became exhausted, but I never considered quitting. I did consider going up to the road, but not seeing a clear path, I soon gave up on that idea. Besides, I could hear cars going by all the time, and someone from the Children's Home might spot me.

After what seemed like a very long time, I rounded a bend, and off in the distance I saw the top of a bridge. Towering behind one side of the bridge was a large rocky cleft. The other side was wide open. It was the passageway into Chester Bowl. I continued walking, and when I got closer, I came to a Y in the trail. One path went up a steep embankment; the other twisted down toward the creek and the bridge.

Was there a way under this bridge, I wondered? From where I stood, it looked similar to the Fourth Street Bridge. It had the same rock architecture and an arched opening in the center, and I knew you couldn't walk under that bridge because a steel gate blocked the entrance. Not wanting to climb the steep embankment, I chose the path to the creek. If nothing else, I could always backtrack. As I got closer, I noticed that it went right up to the side of the opening and from there it dropped sharply down onto another path that led directly into a tunnel under the bridge. I followed it to the opening and peered inside. It was dark and cold in there, and a draft of damp air chilled me.

Suddenly, I heard footsteps from somewhere behind me, and I almost jumped out of my skin. A young man jogging toward me said, "Hey, you're a little young to be out here by yourself! Are you lost?"

"No! Is that the way to the ski lifts?"

"That it be! Just follow me and you'll run right into Chester Bowl and the ski lifts." He jogged past me into the tunnel, and I heard the echo of his footsteps as he receded into the darkness. Determined to see this through, I again peered inside and there, to my relief, I saw his silhouette against the sun filtering in from the far side.

For years, I told people that I had walked through a dark underground sewer on my journey to St. Scholastica, but the only thing on the route I took that even resembles a sewer is the walkway under that bridge. Maybe it was the combination of the darkness, the clamminess of the cool, wet, confined space, and the moldy smell of wet rock and dirt that made my imagination play tricks on me. Whatever it was, I got through the tunnel unharmed and eventually stepped into the sunlight on the other side.

After my eyes had adjusted to the bright sun, I saw before me an expansive bowl-shaped valley with tree-covered slopes on all sides. To my right, an elevated road ran into the valley and directly in front of me, a couple and their two young children were sitting at one of several picnic tables arranged randomly on the grassy knoll that sloped down to the creek. A hundred yards or so beyond them, the creek widened, creating a large pond. To the right of that stood the skating shack. I couldn't see the ski jump from where I stood, but I knew from having been to the park before that it was up the hill and to the left of the pond. I ran up to the couple and said, "Excuse me. Do you know where St. Scholastica is?"

"I do," the man answered. "You take Skyline Drive to Kenwood and…"

"Someone told me it was behind the ski lift," I interrupted.

"Oh, you mean you want to *walk* to St. Scholastica."

"Yes."

"Well, I don't think there is a trail that will take you there, at least none that I know of. The river that runs through the college drains into Chester Creek, but I don't even know where it's at and I'm pretty sure there's no path."

"Can't I walk up the hill by the ski jump?" I asked. I was determined to follow through with my quest, and if that meant hiking into the unknown, then so be it.

"Isn't it behind the Bobsled Run?" the woman asked.

"Where is the Bobsled Run?" I asked, not wanting to lose momentum, while keeping them from asking me why I wanted to know.

"The Bobsled Run is on the other side of the ski lift," the man said. "It ends at the creek in that open field beyond the skating shack. You can't see the run from here, but I think you'll be able to see it when you get to that open field. Do you understand what I'm saying?"

"I think so," I answered, hesitantly. "Do I follow it to the top?"

"I think he has to keep to the right of the Bobsled run," the woman cut in.

"I think you're right, honey," the man said. "OK. Here's what you do. Go to where the Bobsled Run ends and then as you walk up the hill keep veering to the right and away from the run. The college is the only building up there, and you'll know when you see it because it has a big lawn in front and the buildings are large. Does that make sense?"

"I think so," I said, uncertain about his directions but anxious to get going.

"Good luck! I hope you don't get lost!" the woman shouted.

[I've often wondered why they didn't ask me what I was doing or why I was alone. The same thing had happened when I ran away from the Children's Home three years earlier. I guess the answer is simple. Adults are reluctant to get involved with someone else's children. Maybe it's only those with the wrong motives who bother to ask questions.]

It was a long walk from the entrance of the bowl to the field on the far side of the park. There weren't that many people around, which was a good thing because no one was there to stop or question me.

When I reached the spot the man had directed me to, I saw, across the creek, a wooden trough winding its way down the hill. This must be the Bobsled Run they were talking about. It looked like a longer and wider version of one of those old water troughs used by miners back in the gold rush days. As there wasn't a crossing at that spot, I backtracked to a bridge at the foot of the ski lifts and then I climbed the hill. If there was a path from Chester Bowl to the college in 1953, I didn't find it, but I did as the couple had told me. I kept the Bobsled Run to my left, veering to my right. The hill was steep, but the going was surprisingly easy. There was a sprinkling of small saplings, but not enough to hamper my progress. I would stop now and then to get my bearings and to listen for cars or other signs of life, but I don't recall ever being afraid. Maybe a little nervous, because I didn't know what lay on the other side of the woods, but as long as I could see the valley, I knew that I could always turn around and go back.

As I neared the top of the hill, the terrain began to level off. I was still going uphill, but it wasn't as steep, and I noticed that the forest was becoming more dense—the trees were not as far apart and there were more of them. Alarmed, I looked behind me and I noticed for the first time that I could no longer see the valley. I was alone, isolated from everyone and everything. Undaunted by this change in circumstances, I kept forging ahead until finally I heard the sound of cars, and then through the trees I saw the road. I quickened my pace and approached it, my energy and resolve renewed.

When I neared the side of the road, I looked for the college, but to my disappointment all I could see were trees, trees, and more trees. Should I go to the right or to the left? Left seemed the *logical* choice because I felt that, if anything, I might have walked too far to the right. Over the years, I've often felt the presence of angels, and I count this as one of those moments, because instead of using logic, I listened to that little voice inside of me that said, "Keep going to the right" even though it meant going back into the woods. Within minutes, I lost sight of the road and the sound of passing cars receded until all I could hear were the rustling of leaves and a chorus of chirping birds.

After what seemed like forever, I heard the sounds of water. I recalled the man saying something about the creek running through the college, so I picked up my pace. Eventually, I came to the water, but it was only a trickle, not the rushing water I was used to seeing in Chester Creek. I was standing on the side of a steep embankment with thick undergrowth everywhere. Realizing that it would be almost impossible for me to climb the steep incline, I retraced my steps until I found a route that looked passable, and then I literally pulled myself up the embankment by hanging on to the slender trunks of saplings growing on the side of the hill. As I neared the crest, I again heard the sound of cars. When I finally reached the top, I saw a highway and across from that, spread out like an alluvial fan, a well-groomed lawn. In the distance, a large building lay against a wooded backdrop.

I had found the Saint Something or Other. Now, all I had to do was find my mother.

CHAPTER 44
The Sisters

I stood at the side of the road and breathed a deep sigh of relief. I don't know how long it actually took, but for a seven-year-old, the walk from the orphanage to the college had been a long-drawn-out journey, filled with anxiety and uncertainty. And it wasn't over yet. I still had to find and confront my mother. What if she wasn't there, and even if she was, did she really have my knife, or had Mrs. Hemphill just made that story up?

Brushing leaves and dirt off my shirt, I looked both ways, and seeing no cars, I scurried across the road and headed for the Y-shaped driveway leading up to the buildings. When I came to the split, I hesitated. My first thought was to just cross the lawn and enter through the door in the center, but then I spotted a man walking to his car. I ran towards him, hoping to catch him before he could drive off, but to my relief, instead of getting into his car, he walked to the back and opened the trunk. I quickened my pace and reached his side just as he was about to close the trunk. Exhausted and out of breath, I shouted, "Mister, do you know where the kitchens are?"

"Sure. You can come in with me. I'll take you there after I drop this off," he said, holding up a box.

"OK," I said.

"If you don't want to wait, you could probably find it yourself. All you have to do is walk behind Tower Hall," he said, pointing toward the building in front of us. "When you get to the other side, you'll see the loading dock in the center and there'll probably be some big trucks parked in front of it. The doors to the kitchen are on the dock. So, what do you want to do? Do you want to come with me or do you think you could find it yourself?"

"I think I can find it," I answered. I wasn't completely comfortable with his directions but I didn't want to wait either so I thanked him and left.

"Well, good luck, young man," I heard him say as I ran off. "You'll probably run into someone else when you get back there. If you get lost, just ask them."

I followed his directions and as soon as I rounded the corner of Tower Hall, I saw a large parking lot between Tower Hall and another building to my right. The lot sloped towards a far-off connecting building in the center, and in front of that was the loading dock. The doors to the kitchen were behind the platform, and together the buildings formed a perfect U. Several semi-trucks were parked in front of the dock, but I didn't see any movement. I climbed the stairs on one end of the dock, went down a cement walkway, and entered the kitchen through a set of swinging double doors. A cool breeze hit me as I entered a darkened space. I heard the swish of water and the bang of metal on metal, like someone was washing pots and pans. I went through another set of swinging doors into a large room that was heavy with the smell of food. It was filled with racks of cooking utensils and rows of tables and chairs. Women in black and white flowing gowns, their heads covered by miniature versions of their gowns, were preparing food.

"Are you lost?"

Startled, I turned and saw a woman dressed in those same black-and-white garments.

"I want to see my mom. They said she's here."

I looked into her round face, but her age and features were mostly hidden by the miniature dress she wore on her head.

"Who is *they*?" she asked in a kind but firm voice.

"Miss Hemphill."

"And who is Miss Hemphill?"

"She's at the Children's Home,"

"I see. Is she the woman in charge?"

"I think so," I answered, confused by her choice of words. "She's the boss of everyone."

"So you came all the way from the Children's Home to see your mom. How did you get here?"

"I walked up the hill by where they ski."

"By yourself? No one came with you?"

"No."

"Who is your mom?"

"Eileen Haataja."

The sister gave me a concerned look. Meanwhile, several other sisters, dressed in the same black-and-white robes, had gathered around us.

"Who is he?" one of them asked.

"He's Eileen's boy," she answered softly.

"Is she here?" I asked eagerly. The way she said, "He's Eileen's boy" gave me reason to hope.

"We'll send someone to find her," she finally answered. "It might be a few minutes. Can you wait right here?"

I nodded, and she signaled for one of the sisters to join her. They talked in private for a few moments, and then the other sister left.

I wish I could remember the names of the sisters who introduced themselves, but I can't. There were too many. Not only that, they all looked the same and they all seemed to have two names like Sister Rose Marie or Sister Ann Marie or Sister Angela something or other. The sister who spoke to me first must have been in charge, because she kept giving everyone else orders. "Why is everyone wearing the same kind of clothes?" I asked her.

"Because we're Sisters of the Order of St. Benedictine and this is our habit. I mean, these are the clothes we wear to show that we belong to the same order." I didn't understand what she meant by *order*, but before I could ask, she said, "I bet you're hungry. Why don't you sit at that table over there, and we'll fix you something to eat."

"What would you like?" one of the younger women asked me. "We're having turkey and mashed potatoes for dinner today. Does that sound good, or would you prefer a nice peanut butter and jelly sandwich with some milk and cookies?"

"A peanut butter and jelly sandwich with cookies!"

"OK," said the head sister, "while we wait for your food, tell us all about your adventure, and don't leave anything out. How did you walk all the way from the Children's Home?"

"Is that the home on Fifteenth Street and Fifth Avenue?" another sister asked.

"I don't know," I answered, not understanding streets and

avenues.

"Is it across from Chester Park?"

"Yes," I answered, recognizing the landmark.

"Did you walk up the road?"

"What road did you take?"

"Did someone drive you?"

"Do they know you're gone?"

The questions flew at me from all directions. Finally the head sister asked, "You didn't follow Chester Creek, did you?"

"Yes. Well, not all the way."

So I told them everything: how my knife had been taken away, how I learned about St. Scholastica, how someone had given me directions, and how I walked from the Home to their kitchens. I talked on and on, stopping only to take a bite from my sandwich or a drink of milk. Other sisters joined us, each wanting to hear the story from beginning to end.

At last one of the sisters said, "Here's Eileen." I turned to see my mother walking down the center aisle. She and the sister who had brought her to me stood in sharp contrast to each other: the sister in her flowing black-and-white habit and my mother in a flower-patterned, knee-length dress, an apron tied tightly around her waist. She wore white socks with brown ox-fords, a combination popular in the '40s and '50s and one that I have always associated with her.

She looked rested, but different somehow; her curly brown hair, shorter than she normally wore it, was combed back behind her ears. Her face, rounder and perhaps a little fuller, looked clean and fresh, but the thing that really struck me was the fullness of her figure. It's hard to describe, but it looked like she had gained some weight: her hips a little wider, her stomach extended, her breasts maybe a little fuller. She wasn't fat-heavy, just different-heavy.

When my mother was maybe twenty feet away from me, she stopped and put both hands to her mouth. "Oh, my, I'm not supposed to see you!" she exclaimed. At first, I thought she was going to turn and leave. Perhaps the sister hadn't told her why she had been summoned, or maybe they wanted to make my presence a surprise. Either way, it left her speechless.

Her words and how she said them struck me as odd at the time, but I didn't give them much weight or thought. Later, of course, I would learn that she had already signed away her parental rights, and the courts had advised her not to see us.

Before my mother could say anything else, the head sister intervened. "Eileen," she said, "isn't this nice? Your son walked all the way from the Children's Home to visit you, and he's been entertaining us with his exploits. Why don't you sit down and visit with him for a while, and we'll talk later about what has to happen."

Mom walked over to the table and sat down opposite me. We didn't hug or kiss, and I didn't rush to her as most kids do when seeing their mother after a long absence. Instead, we just looked at each other while I kept eating my sandwich.

"How did you get here, Terry?" she asked, her voice low and almost timid.

"I walked."

"You walked all the way from the Children's Home? Terry, you could have been hurt or gotten lost!" she said, increasingly concerned.

"I didn't get lost," I said, taking a bite of my sandwich.

She hadn't asked why I had come, and for some reason it didn't seem to matter—the food and the excitement of talking to the sisters were taking up most of my time and my thoughts.

"How did you find out where I was?"

"Miss Hemphill told me."

"Does she know you're here?"

"I don't know."

I explained how I had found out where she was and how I had walked from the orphanage to the college. She sat riveted to her seat, staring at me intently; several of the sisters stood nearby, occasionally reminding me of any details I had left out.

By the time I finished the story, only the crusts remained on the plate, and most of the sisters had gone off to prepare the noon meal. Only the head sister and two others remained.

"Why don't you show Terry your room, Eileen?" said the head sister.

"Are you sure? I'm supposed to help with the meal."

"This is a time that God has made for you to be with your son. I think we can get along without you for the time being." The sister bent over and whispered something into my mother's ear, and then she said, "OK! The two of you run along, and we'll send someone to get you when it's time for Terry to go. Terry, you know we have to call the Children's Home to let them know you're here, don't you?" I did understand, and I nodded to let her know.

"Thank you, Sister," my mother said.

"Terry, would you like to see my room?" she asked, motioning for me to follow. All I could think was, "Do we have to do this? Just ask her for the knife and get it over with!" but I kept silent as I anxiously followed her out the back door and into more uncertainty.

CHAPTER 45
The Room

As we stepped onto the loading dock, I almost lost my balance. It wasn't because of anything in my path—it was from the shock of the sunlight combined with the disappearance of the trucks that had been there earlier. The area that had been confining and crowded on my arrival was now open and spacious, giving me the sensation of falling. The feeling left quickly, and my mother broke the silence. "I live over there, above the garage." The structure she pointed at was the other building connected to the dock. It looked older than Tower Hall, which was made of brick. Its walls were dark granite boulders held together with light tan cement, making it look like a nineteenth-century prison.

"It's not much, I know, but I don't spend a lot of time there," she said. "They keep me busy, and when I do have free time I usually walk in the flower garden behind the college. It's called Mary's Gardens. I think that's the name of the sister who started the garden, but I'm not sure. Would you like to see the garden after you've seen my room?"

I nodded yes and followed her inside. After my eyes adjusted to the darkness, I saw that we were in a narrow passageway. The paint on the wooden staircase was cracked and peeling, and the boards creaked and echoed as we climbed. At the end of a dark corridor were two dimly visible doors.

"Which one is yours?" I don't know why I even asked. I just wanted to leave. There was something about the place that made me feel uncomfortable. Not for me, but for my mother.

"It's the room on the right at the far end. I know it's not much, but it will do for the time being, until I can afford to live in a real house and have my own furniture."

I cringed. My mother always talked about *someday*: someday we'll be a family, someday we'll have our own house, someday this, someday that. My heart sank, and I wanted to shout, "Stop saying that! I hate it! It's not going to happen and you know it!" but I didn't. Would someday ever come for her? Does she even know about the adoption plans?

Her room was small—no bigger than a jail cell. It contained only a single bed, an old standup dresser, and one chair alone in the corner. The walls were a dull white. Several cracks ran spiderweb-like from the ceiling to the bare floor, which was worn and unvarnished like the stairs and the floor in the hallway. The only ornaments were a faded and warped picture of Jesus above the dresser, plain white curtains on two small windows, and a crucifix above the bed. There were no pictures of us.

"Can I have my knife back?" I asked, suddenly wanting to get this over with.

"Your knife?" she asked in obvious bewilderment. "What knife are you talking about?"

"The knife Dad gave me last year! Remember?"

"I'm sorry. I don't have it, and I don't remember. What kind of knife was it?

"The Jim Bowie knife with the white handle, and it went in a leather thing. You know!" I was starting to get irritated.

Suddenly the truth hit me. Of course she didn't know! Dad had given it to me in private. What was it he had said? "If you tell them what happened, they won't let your mother see you anymore."

"Miss Hemphill said you came by the Children's Home last winter and she gave it to you!" I said, getting louder by the second. I faltered. "Forget it. I don't need it anyway. My new mom and dad will give me a knife."

"Oh! You know that I'm not your mom anymore?" she asked, stunned.

"Miss Hemphill told me she found a new mom and dad for Jean and me and we're going to meet them in a couple of days," I said hesitantly, suddenly very much aware of her discomfort.

"That soon? Oh, my," she cried, her hand going up to her throat.

"Larry was just adopted, and he's already gone to his new home."

"No," she said, her voice now soft and forlorn, "they didn't tell me. They haven't told me anything since I… " Her words trailed off.

At the time, I didn't know what she meant and I didn't think to ask, but now, of course, I know that she had started to say, "I signed the release papers."

"I don't want to be in this room anymore," I said, feeling desperate. I pitied her, and although pity might be a form of love, it is not the kind of emotion a child should feel about their mother.

"OK, she said. "Do you want me to take you back to the kitchen?" At this point, I think that even she was having regrets about our reunion—at least the part about going to her room.

"No, but I don't want to be in *here*. I don't like it here."

"All right, I'll show you the garden. It's peaceful there. I go there when I need to be alone."

I nodded, and sighed in relief as we stepped into the sunlight. I reluctantly followed her to the back of the building. I was about to make a promise that would have a profound impact on both of our lives.

CHAPTER 46

The Promise

My mother took me to a narrow dirt road that took us behind the building she lived in and to the back of the college. The first thing I spotted as we stepped onto the road was a glass building. Having never seen one, I asked my mother what it was and she said, "It's a greenhouse; they grow flowers there."

Confused, I asked, "Is that the flower garden?"

"No. The flower garden is up ahead."

"How come they have a garden if they grow flowers inside that house?"

"That's so the sisters can have flowers in their rooms all year round."

"Oh," I said, not understanding why someone would want flowers in the winter, but I didn't press the issue. That was their business. I had my own worries to think about.

We climbed an incline, and at the top the road split into a Y at the edge of a large flat field with white lines drawn across it.

"Would you like to walk to the cemetery instead of the garden?" My mother asked, pulling me away from my thoughts.

"Will it take a long time?"

"Well, it's a lot further then the garden, but I walk to the cemetery all the time. I like to read the headstones, and it'll give us more time together." Just what I didn't want, I thought, more time together, and why would she take me to a cemetery anyway? Cemeteries have dead people in them, and why would anyone want to read headstones?

By this time, I was really beginning to have second thoughts about being with my mother. I just wanted to go back to the Children's Home. Running away had been an adventure and the sisters had made me feel wanted, but being with my mother was beginning to drain me. I felt sorry for this woman who wouldn't be my mother anymore—this woman who I still loved in a hopeless sort of way. I had been her firstborn—her little man—and even though she might not have been the best mother in the world, we had formed a bond. I wanted her to hold my hand, to kiss and hug me, and tell me that everything would be all right, but at this stage in my life, I felt more secure and comfortable at the orphanage. I wanted to yell, "Why can't you take care of us! What's wrong with you!" but that would have been wrong, and I knew it.

"Where is it?" I asked.

"The cemetery?"

"Yes."

"It's on the other side of the soccer field," she said, pointing across the open space.

"No!" I said abruptly. "I don't want to go that far." I had already spent most of the day walking. The last thing I needed was another long walk.

"That's OK, I'll show you the garden. It's beautiful at this time of the year."

She guided me though an opening in a hedge and into a field filled with flowers. A well-worn path crisscrossed the garden, widening in front of a statue. "Isn't this beautiful?" she asked. "I think it's the most beautiful place in the world. I come here every afternoon to relax. Well, not *every* afternoon. Sometimes I take the bus and go shopping or to your Aunt Irene's, but after my noon chores are done, I love to come here and sit and look at the flowers. I even know their names. Would you like me to tell you about them?" I nodded listlessly.

As we walked, she provided an exotic name for each of the different colored plants. I don't remember the names, and flowers were the last thing on my mind. I wanted to talk about what had happened. Why hadn't we seen her for almost a year? How could someone just stop being your mom? Instead, she talked on and on about the plants, about a priest who came there on a certain day of the week to pray, and a sister who took care of the garden. We stopped in front of two statues. She gave each a name, going into detail about their origin and meaning.

"Why aren't you going to be our mom anymore?" I finally blurted.

She stopped walking and, looking down at me with great pain in her face, said, "When I signed the papers, they said I wasn't supposed to see you anymore."

What papers? I thought. What did papers have to do with her not being my mom?

"I don't know how to tell you this," she continued, her voice almost inaudible. "It's complicated and it involves your dad and other things that are not easy to talk about."

Spit it out! I thought. I wanted to shake her and tell her that I didn't care about my dad or about *complicated*, whatever that meant. I just wanted to know why she wasn't going to be my mom. How could your mom not be your mom anymore? That was stupid.

Then she shifted gears, her voice returning from *lost* to somewhere between doom and gloom. "It won't be long now, Terry, before someone comes to pick you up. Let's sit down," she said, pointing at a granite bench that sat in the grass across the road from the garden. "We can see the parking lot from there."

Neither of us said a word as we crossed to the bench. While in the process of sitting down, I looked up and saw a black sedan at the far end of the parking lot. Its doors were wide open and people were standing close by having what appeared to be an animated conversation. I knew they were there for me.

One of the sisters standing next to the car looked up, saw us, and yelled. "They're here, Eileen. I'm sorry, but Terry will have to go."

"Oh," my mother sighed, lifting her hand to her mouth, "so soon already."

I slid down from the bench and faced her.

"*Why aren't you going to be my mom anymore?*"

"I'm sorry, Terry, that I haven't been a good mother. I love you. I will always love you, and I'll pray for you every day. Please tell Jean that I love her, and be nice to your new mom and dad."

For the first time, I started to cry. "Why can't you still be my mom? How come I have to have a new mom?"

"Because I can't take care of you and I don't have a place for us to live. I tried to be a good mom, but nothing's gone right. I will always think about you, wherever you are. Remember that."

"When I get bigger I'll come back and find you, you wait

and see!" I said, tears streaming down my face. We embraced and held each other for a long time. I had never seen her cry, I mean *really* cry, and it was a first for me too. I knew deep in the pit of my stomach that it was over. She wasn't my mom anymore.

"Eileen!" someone shouted. "Terry has to go now. I'm sorry, but they're waiting."

Finally, she pushed me away and, after wiping the tears from my face, said, "You're my brave little man. I hope you do come back someday. I'll be waiting for you. Take care of Jean and try to find Larry too. He should be with the two of you."

"I don't want to go. Please don't make me! Come with me!" I beseeched, taking her hand.

"No, I need to stay here," she said somberly, pulling her hand out of mine. I can't keep you. They won't let me. You have to be strong and go by yourself. Please, don't make this any harder than you have to. You come back and find me when you get older, but now you have to go, because I don't think I can take this any longer."

As I walked toward the waiting car, I heard her say, "Terry." I turned and looked at her. "I might have to leave here."

"How come?"

"Because I've. . . done something. I don't think they will let me stay here much longer. But I'll stay in Duluth. When you return you'll be able to find me in the telephone directory, OK?"

I nodded. I didn't know what she meant by a telephone directory, but I had found her this time, hadn't I? I could find her again, and I'd be all grown up the next time.

I suppose that I could have made a scene, but something inside me told me that it was over. She *wasn't* my mom anymore.

She hadn't been my mom for a long time, and I needed to go on with my life. When I looked back for the last time, I saw her still sitting on the bench, head bowed, hands on her lap, shoulders shaking. Right then and there I made up my mind that I would come back and find her when I got older, but I knew even then that we would never be a real family.

Back at the orphanage, I wasn't disciplined, and I didn't even receive a lecture. It was getting late and I was tired, so I ate and went to bed. The next day, our new mom and dad arrived. After the formal introductions were made, they took us to, you guessed it, Chester Bowl for a picnic, and we sat at the very table the young couple had sat at the day before. During one of those embarrassing pauses that I suspect is common in situations like this, I gazed up at the wooded hills, knowing that my mother was up there somewhere. I wondered what her life would be like without her "brave little man," but this reflection quickly passed and I returned to my future. Two days later, Jean and I left the Children's Home to begin our new lives.

Our new parents, Walter and Winifred Degner. Photo taken on the way to our new home.

VII: THE FUNERAL PART VII: THE FUNERA

The author's family at Cook, Minnesota - 2006

CHAPTER 47

A Family Gathering

Cook, Minnesota, August 21, 2006. "Good morning. Most of you have never seen me before, but there's a good chance Alan told you about me due to the unique circumstances surrounding our relationship. I'm his nephew Terry. These are my children and grandchildren sitting in the front pew, and behind them are my sister Jean and her family."

My family and I were attending the funeral of Alan Larson, who had suddenly died of a heart attack on the sidewalk in front of his optometrist's office.

"Alan was one of the most loving men I've ever known," I said, tears welling in my eyes, a lump in my throat. "He cared about his family and he proved by his actions that he wanted to be a part of my family. To this end, he would drive hundreds of miles to attend my children's graduation ceremonies, weddings, and baptisms. When we went on our annual camping trips, he and his wife Lois would drive to our campsite, and we would sit around the campfire talking and laughing into the night."

I stopped and wiped the tears from my eyes. "I'm sorry," I said, choking on my words. "I've never experienced anything like this before." Looking down at Alan's wife Lois, at my daughters and their families, and at my wife, I took courage, and after taking a deep breath, I continued, "I'm the eldest son of Alan's sister Eileen. Eileen had three children. Besides me, there's my sister Jean and a younger brother by the name of Larry, who's not here. I lived with Alan and his parents, Nels and Lillian, for three of the first four years of my life. This ended in 1950 when our mother placed us in an orphanage. Three years later, we were adopted, and I didn't see Alan for the next eighteen years. Then, in July of 1971, I returned to Cook, and Alan has been an important member of our family ever since."

I went on to explain the events leading up to our reunion. I told the congregation the story of how I found Aunt Margaret: the waitress at the restaurant, the knock on Margaret's door, and the shock of learning that she was my grandmother's sister.

Then I told them about how I met Alan. "Margaret told me that Alan lived right here in town." I said. "She asked me if I remembered him. I knew that if I were going to get a word in edgewise, I would have to talk quickly." Another low murmur. "Yup, I told her, I have more memories of Alan then I have of anyone else. He was my boyhood idol. I wanted to be just like him. Once, after Grandma cut my hair, my mother said, 'You look just like your Uncle Alan.' Expecting a miraculous transformation, I begged her to lift me up to the mirror on the dining room wall. To my disappointment, however, all I saw was this little boy with blond hair and big dimples—not the ruggedly handsome man my uncle was."

'Well, I'm sure he'd love to see you,' Margaret told me, 'and you'll like him. Everyone in town likes Alan. I don't think he's ever had a bad word said about him. He lives just on the other side of town. I don't know if he's home now, but if you follow this street,' she said, pointing east, 'it will take you right to his house. It's the blue one on the other side of the high school'."

That's how I found Alan and how we became a family again. Thank you, Lois," I said, looking down at her, "for sharing your husband with us for all these years," and with that I went back to my seat.

Alan had chosen to be cremated, so we didn't drive to the cemetery, but I did help carry his casket to the traditional waiting hearse. Afterwards I said to my sister, "He's the last one, Jean. We're the next generation to go."

She laughed, "Yes, makes you feel old, doesn't it?"

"Well, we still have lots of years left, and with all these grandchildren to keep us busy," I said, motioning at the children milling around us, "we won't get bored."

"Isn't that the truth." she replied with a chuckle. "Dwaine and I never have any time to ourselves. If we aren't working, we're off watching the kids in sports or theater. It's a crazy schedule, but we love it."

"Well, I'm in the same boat, and I wouldn't change it for anything. Have you ever been to our mom's grave?"

"No," she answered. "We've only been here once before, and that was a long time ago. Uncle Alan always came to our house for special occasions. Is she buried close by?"

"It's about a mile from here and on the way to the farm. Let's stop at the cemetery first, and then we'll show the kids the farm."

I had visited Mom's gravesite several times over the years. Alan had buried her next to her parents in a cemetery on the outskirts of Cook. There is no headstone proclaiming her earthly existence—no "Here lies the daughter of…" homage—only a small, ground-level stone with the inscription "Eileen Haataja, 1924–1967."

"Wow, she was only forty-two when she died," one of my sons-in-law said as we gathered around the stone. "I've heard bits and pieces of what happened, but not the whole story. Why did she take her own life?"

"Well, to make a long story short," I said, "over the years, my father kept asking my mother for a divorce, and she kept refusing. Then, in 1966, for unknown reasons, she granted it. According to Alan and his sisters, shortly before my mother's death on January 20, 1967, my father *bragged* to her—that was the word they used—that he had known of my whereabouts for some time, and that he had been keeping track of me. Unfortunately, that wasn't all he told her. To make matters worse, he told her I had died in a car accident—*killed* is the word he actually used."

"Oh my gosh, that's terrible!" my oldest granddaughter gasped.

"Yes, it is," I said. "According to Alan and his sisters, it wasn't long after this that she took her own life."

"How did it happen?" another son-in-law asked.

"She took an overdose of sleeping pills and died on the way to the hospital, and according to Alan, she left a note on the nightstand that said, "I can't live without my children. No hope."

"Wow, that's a sad story," the son-in-law replied. "I can't imagine ever doing something like that to another human being."

For several moments, no one said a word. Then Jean broke

the silence. "I don't know if I've ever told you this, Terry, but Alan said something to me that I thought was strange, especially coming from him."

"What was that?" I asked.

"He said her death was probably for the best. In his opinion, she was a very needy woman."

"Yes, he was probably right," I said, rolling my eyes and nodding. "I think she *was* needy, but that's not the issue. First, she didn't deserve what happened to her, and second, she shouldn't have given up hope. Look at what she missed!" I said, gesturing at what could have been her *real family*.

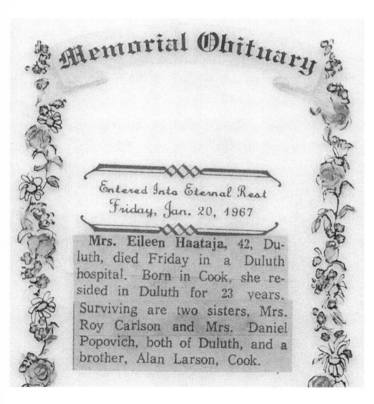

Memorial Obituary

Entered Into Eternal Rest
Friday, Jan. 20, 1967

Mrs. Eileen Haataja, 42, Duluth, died Friday in a Duluth hospital. Born in Cook, she resided in Duluth for 23 years. Surviving are two sisters, Mrs. Roy Carlson and Mrs. Daniel Popovich, both of Duluth, and a brother, Alan Larson, Cook.

CHAPTER 48
The Rest of the Story

Eden Prairie, Minnesota, 2011. Over the years, relatives and friends have encouraged me to write this, my memoir, but what many of them do not know is that at the age of twelve I made a solemn promise to God that I would undertake this task when I reached my senior years. The inspiration came from the author Charles Dickens, especially from his portraits of street urchins and orphans. I started reading his novels in the fourth grade, and I couldn't put them down until I had read all of them, or at least all of the ones I could find in the school library.

As I was getting close to completing the manuscript, some of my friends asked if I had learned anything about myself that I did not know before I undertook the journey. The answer is yes and no: no, because the pieces of the puzzle had been lying around for years in plain sight, and yes, because I had never taken the time to assemble them into a cohesive whole.

What was I like during those difficult years? Or maybe the

question should be, what was my personality like, from a self-perspective? I was an overly sensitive child and I took rejection by my peers, especially attacks on my self-esteem, very personally. I believe that I was probably born with that personality (it wasn't an acquired trait) and that the orphanage experience (abandonment) exacerbated the sense of rejection I felt when peers said or did things that were disparaging. The superficial symptom of feeling rejected was anger, and the physical component was fighting. I got into lots of physical fights as a child, which carried over into adulthood. As my adopted mother told me once, "you look like you have the weight of the world weighing on your shoulders."

To offset these negatives, I was blessed with some gifts that kept me from drifting to the dark side, to use an expression from *Star Wars*. First, unlike the Steven I wrote about in the book, I had a conscience, and I never acted with malicious intent. My intent was not to harm but to protect, which makes sense if you think about it. Second, whenever my actions were wrong, and there were times when I made mistakes, I would quickly apologize. It was not unusual for me to tell someone I was sorry even before the person realized something had happened. Third, I was small for my age, and cute. When I got into physical fights, it was with bullies, and they were always bigger or there were more of them. For these reasons, I never got into serious trouble.

Hate is another one of those deep-seated afflictions that I was fortunate enough to escape. It would have been easy for me to hate my father, but I can't recall ever feeling that way about him—or about anyone, for that matter. There had been times when he frightened me, and some of his traits were repulsive, but I didn't hate him for it. My own struggles have taught me that the more you know about someone, the easier it is to accept them for what they are. Besides, my situation improved after I left the orphanage. I don't often speak for my sister, but I think I can safely say that she believes, like me, that God's hand was on us during those difficult times, and that what happened, happened for the best. It's hard for me to imagine where I would be today if not for the adoption, but we both know with certainty that it would be a far darker place.

That said, I feel compelled to put into writing some of the more important facts and underlying details that I gathered, because if you are like me, you too want to know what took place "behind the scenes." Many of the facts and details support the material in this, my memoir, but some are outside the scope of the main narrative, including one rather shocking surprise that I alluded to towards its end.

Before I do, I'd like to thank my adoptive mother, who has been so gracious throughout this process. I did have concerns about what finding my biological mother would do to the woman who cared for me from the age of eight (one month shy of eight to be exact) until I graduated from high school and whom I will always call Mother. My adoptive father passed away in 1967, so he was out of the picture by the time I started my search, but I wanted to make sure my adoptive mother understood that our relationship would never change. To this end, I kept her in the loop at every stage. To her credit, she responded by graciously including Alan and the two sisters into our family, and they responded in kind.

Was I indirectly responsible for Eileen's suicide? That's a question I've asked myself repeatedly since the day I learned of her fate. The circumstances surrounding Eileen Haataja's death are interesting, to say the least. When I first learned of her death, I was somewhat stunned, but I must admit that I didn't feel particularly anguished or grief-stricken. In fact, if anything, I might have felt a slight sense of relief. Yes, I had promised her I would return, but I had some real misgivings about what it would be like to meet her after all those years. Would she throw herself at me, would she cling to me and become a financial burden, or would she be indifferent and reject me?

Margaret told me that Eileen had committed suicide, but she didn't provide any details because I don't think she was ever told the facts. It was Alan and his sisters who did that, and as I would later learn, their interpretation didn't fit all of the facts either. According to them, Eileen committed suicide shortly after Nels fed her the story about my death in a car accident, leaving the note that said, "I can't live without my children. No hope." They didn't provide a copy of the note or any facts to back up their story, and so, wanting to take them at their word, I let it ride. However, I did learn something early on in my investigation that I should have paid more attention to, and that concerns a man by the name of Vic.

On a return visit to Duluth in the mid-1970s, I tracked down a woman by the name of Mary Alfonsi. Mary had worked with Eileen at the Afterno Nursing Home in Duluth. According to Mary, "Eileen fell in love with a married man from Michigan by the name of Vic. His wife and children lived in Michigan, and he travelled back and forth between that state and Duluth on a freighter." I got the distinct impression that Mary didn't particularly like this man, and her attitude didn't improve as she described the relationship. "Vic fed your mother a line about getting a divorce so they could be together, but after they came back from a vacation in Las Vegas, he told your mother he couldn't divorce his wife because he was Catholic." In Mary's opinion, Vic may have been the reason why Eileen committed suicide.

Her words didn't register with me until I requested and received a copy of the coroner's report. This occurred after Alan's death. In it the coroner wrote, "A note, which is filed with the case report says, 'I can't live without my children. No hope. I loved you Vic.'"

Alan and his sisters never mentioned a boyfriend or anyone by the name of Vic. It's possible they never knew him and that they never saw the suicide note, but I have a hunch they did. Nothing specific, but I recall overhearing one of the sisters ask if Vic was at Eileen's funeral. It was a private conversation, and it struck me as odd at the time, but I didn't say anything, and the moment passed.

The coroner's report goes on to say that on January 20, 1967, Eileen Haataja took her own life in the service quarters of the Afterno Nursing Home. She "overdosed on tranquilizers" and "hit her head alongside a chair, tangling under some electric light wires, and was taken to St. Luke's where she died."

Then another piece of the puzzle fell into place when I requested and received a copy of Nillo (Nels) and Eileen's divorce records. According to the records, the divorce officially took place in August of 1966. Eileen committed suicide on January 20, 1967—approximately six months after the divorce. The siblings said that Nels told Eileen about my death in a car accident "just before" she committed suicide. It's certainly possible that they met and discussed my death shortly before the suicide, but "just before" may have been as much as six months before.

Based on this new information, did Eileen agree to the divorce because of a budding relationship with Vic, and did the subsequent break-up contribute to her suicide? Chances are the answer to both questions is yes. However, I have to believe that the cause for her depression and suicide was more than likely the chain of events that started with the loss of her children, followed by the break-up of a relationship, culminating with the "news" that the one child she counted on to come back and find her was dead.

How did Alan and the sisters react to seeing us after all those years? Alan treated me like a son from the day we met. However, information about the family and Eileen came in bits and pieces; some came willingly, while the rest came more grudgingly. He told me once, "Terry, I don't like talking about the past. I know you want to learn more about your mother, but some things are just too painful to talk about." For this reason, I let Alan move at his own pace and in his own way, and that's why I didn't look up some of the information until after his death—I didn't want to hurt him.

Despite his reluctance to revisit the past, Alan did contribute. It was Alan who gave me the black-and-white photos. I suspect, although he never said it, that they were a part of Eileen's belongings. Most of the locations in the photos were obvious, but some showed us in settings I couldn't place. When I asked Alan about the pictures of us in what I would later learn was Morgan Park, he just shrugged and answered, "I'm not sure where those pictures were taken."

Not long after Alan's funeral, Rhoda's daughter sent me a batch of black-and-whites from her mother's collection. Most were duplicates of the photographs Alan gave me, but on the back were written dates and locations. That's how I came to learn about Morgan Park.

Alan also sent me Eileen's memorial notice and a "This is Your Life" locket that, according to him, Eileen wore on her deathbed. Inside were two photos: one of Jean and me standing in front of a tree at the farm and the other a close-up of Larry. To this day, lipstick stains are clearly visible on the photos (see back cover).

Over the thirty-plus years that I knew Alan, we probably got together at least twice a year, and sometimes more, but I can count on one hand the number of times I saw Irene and Rhoda. If Alan knew we were coming, he would invite the sisters to join us at his cabin on Lake Vermilion. Sometimes they would show up, but more often than not, they found reasons to excuse themselves. Stranger yet, I was never invited to their homes. Also, unlike Alan, they never came to my children's formal ceremonies, although, in fairness, I hadn't bothered to ask them. When they did show up at the cabin, they were silent and reserved. On the few occasions I talked to them, they were less than forthcoming with answers; at times they were defensive and at other times teary-eyed. According to Jean, whenever she looked at them they would start to cry. I'm sure it was difficult to see us without looking back and wondering what they could have done differently. However, that is a question I've never concerned myself about because Jean and I believe we are far better off with our new life.

Alan never did get around to telling me about Eileen's last will and testament, and Eileen's inheritance from the sale of the farm only came up once. It wasn't a will as such, just a letter and a manila folder filled with her worldly assets. The letter made Alan the executor, instructing him to use the money from her checking account for funeral expenses. On her death, Eileen had $1,034.43 in savings, $560 in checking, and another $4.21 in her wallet. In 1967, you could buy a brand new Chevrolet Camaro for around $2,500, so she had managed to sock away a modest savings. I'm sure that most of the money went for burial expenses and for the small inlaid stone that marks her grave, but I do regret the fact that Alan didn't tell me about the letter and what was in the folder. As for the inheritance, Alan did say once that he wished we could have gotten her share from the sale of the farm. I appreciated his sincerity, and the matter passed without any emotional attachments. I had always found Alan's heart to be in the right place, and I will forever be thankful for his presence in my life.

Was Eileen Haataja retarded or was that my imagination? It is true that when people would ask what my biological mother was like, I would often say, "She wasn't the brightest bulb on the Christmas tree." However, it's one thing to say something like that in private, another to put it into writing. I've thought long and hard about what she was like, and I put off making any hard judgments until I had finished the memoir because I wanted time to weigh all of the facts. I wanted to be fair to her and to myself. I've concluded that "mildly retarded" is perhaps too strong a descriptor for her condition, but from what I remember and from the information I have been able to gather, it's probably close to the truth.

First, Eileen was a blue baby at birth. According to medical records, she was born four hours after her twin sister Irene. I'm no medical expert, but I suspect that oxygen deprivation was the cause of the blueness, and that this may have resulted in some brain damage.

Second, Eileen fell behind her twin sister in school by two full grades: once in grade school and again in ninth grade, and attendance records don't support illness as a cause. The twins also attended separate grade schools. This would be unusual under any circumstances, but in a small community like Cook, it's especially strange. On top of that, Eileen's grades were marked as unaccredited and ungraded while Irene's were both accredited and graded.

Eileen's grades in high school were dismal—a few Fs, lots of Ds, and a scattering of Cs. (Grades, of course, don't necessarily provide a true picture of a person's abilities. One of my classmates in high school failed English four years in a row. He later graduated from New York University.)

Both sisters dropped out of school before they graduated: Irene as a senior in 1942 and Eileen as a junior in 1943. According to Irene's oldest son, his mother dropped out to attend welding school. This was during the war years when women worked in manufacturing plants producing arms and ammunition for the war effort. He also told me that she was ashamed of the poverty she grew up in and she wanted more out of life. Given the fact that they were twins, it would seem reasonable that Eileen would follow the same path after dropping out of school, and photographs seem to back this up. Many of the photos of Eileen taken during that time are of Irene and her in Duluth, and in every instance hair, makeup, and clothing are fashionable for that period.

Lastly, Eileen's employment history suggests a simple, unimaginative existence. From 1951 to 1954 Eileen worked in the kitchens at St. Scholastica for board and room and a little spending money. When I visited the college, one of the sisters who knew Eileen said, "From what I remember, your mother never complained about her work, she was always clean, and she kept to herself most of the time." She added, "I remember that she wasn't a troublemaker," as if some of the help had given them problems.

From the beginning of 1955 to 1957, Eileen lived and worked at the Holland Hotel in Duluth as a housekeeper. Then she worked for nine years as a housekeeper and part-time cook at the Afterno Nursing Home, drawing an average gross income of $165 per month while living in the service quarters. According to the woman who helped me dig through the employment records, Eileen was the only employee on record who lived at the home.

When she signed away her parental rights, Eileen was under heavy sedation and was undergoing shock treatments. Rhoda's daughter saw an official document in her mother's files that testified to this last point, but it has since disappeared, and I have not bothered to look into the matter.

If loving your children is the true measure of motherhood, then Eileen was a good mother. However, I think it would be more accurate to say that she was a loving mother who did not have a support system or the skills to raise three children. She desperately wanted to have a normal family, but her dependence on others made her an easy target for someone like my father.

What happened to Nels Haataja? I invited Nels back into my life in 1975. By then I was out of college, I owned my first home, and I was confident about where my life was headed. I had known for some time where to find him. I first saw his name in the Duluth telephone directory in 1971, and I knew instantly that I had found him, but I also knew with the same amount of certainty that I did not want to see him—not then anyway. When I returned in 1975, his name was gone. There were several Haatajas in the directory but none with the first name of Nels. He had deserted his second family sometime after 1971 and, as he had done with us, fled to Butte, Montana. Instead of contacting them, I called a family with the last name of Haataja in Menahga, Minnesota. A man's voice on the other end of the line said, "Yes, I know where Nels lives," and "I'll give him your message," but he refused to answer any of my questions.

A few days after I left the message, Nels called, and within the month, he and his new wife showed up at my doorstep. It wasn't a happy reunion, but part of that was my fault. I hadn't exactly invited him back into my life to call him dad. I wanted answers and he was the most likely source. Ironically, the first thing he asked as we walked from the car to the house was, "Were you ever in a car accident?" I told him no. When I asked him why he wanted to know, he said, "I was just curious, that's all," and he refused to discuss it further. In fact, when I pushed him for answers about anything to do with the past, he said, "If I had known you were going to ask me all these questions, I wouldn't have come." Because of the way he said it, I felt trapped into treating him with kid gloves for the rest of the visit.

From the moment he arrived, he bragged about this and that, he embellished everything, and every other word was a swear word. He hadn't changed—it felt like old times. Eventually I had to ask him to watch his language in front of my daughter, and he gave me a "Who the hell are you to tell me to watch my mouth" look, and then he said, "I'm sure she'll hear a lot worse by the time she's grown up." My wife and I were both relieved when he left.

Several weeks later, he dropped in unexpectedly on my sister Jean and her family. The one thing that sticks in her memory about that visit is his comment that he would "put her in his will." When she told me about it, we both laughed at its absurdity. It was obvious from the way he spoke and acted that he didn't have a pot to piss in, and even if he did, we had no interest in his money.

I saw him only once after that, but we would sometimes talk by phone. Once in awhile he would send me a postcard or a letter and I would send him photos of my children, but that was the extent of our relationship. In the early 1990s, he called to say that he was "sorry for how things turned out." I accepted his apology. It sounded like he was going through the Twelve Step program and that he had become a born again Christian, so I didn't press him for details on what he meant by "how things turned out." I have often wondered if he ever got around to asking God to forgive him for telling Eileen I was dead.

Nels, I would learn, was the product of rape. At the age of fourteen, his mother, my paternal grandmother, Hilda Johnson Haataja, went to live with and care for her older sister, who had cancer. While there, she had an affair with the sister's husband and got pregnant. The state convicted the husband of rape and deported him to Finland. Grandma went on to marry her high school sweetheart, who later adopted Nels. Together they had fifteen more children. There's another interesting aside to this story. The biological father, the man who raped Hilda, returned to the United State and Nels took care of him during his senior years. Evidently, Nels was under the impression that he would receive a sizable inheritance, but it turned out the man was penniless. The only thing he got for his efforts was the cost of shipping the body back to Finland.

Nels Haataja died in 2002 at the age of 80, but not without fanfare. It seems that after his conversion, he went on to make a good name for himself in the community, and many of his new friends showed up at his funeral to pay their last respects. Some even stood and praised him for the good and kind deeds he had done in the community.

What really happened at the family reunion in 1952? With Nels dead and with the passing of Alan (Rhoda and Irene had already passed away) and with the first draft of this memoir completed, I got more active with my searches, and to my surprise I came across one more shocking discovery. In 2007, a first cousin called. She told me that while rummaging through some of her mother's things, she had run across several items that might be of interest. One was a Final Notice of Commitment form dated July 27, 1956. It read, "Eileen (Larson) Haataja, mother of Keith Allen Haataja, hereby commits Keith Allen Haataja to the guardianship of the Commissioner of Public Welfare of the State of Minnesota." In addition to the form, she found two photos, and in one Eileen is sitting next to a child on an armchair. On the back of the photo are the words, "Keith Allen Haataja, born June 4, 1953." This information hit me like a sledgehammer. When I asked the cousin if her mother had ever mentioned another child, she said, "No, she never said anything about Eileen having another son."

It was for that reason, more than anything else, that I requested the copy of Nels and Eileen's divorce papers. The grounds for divorce were "non-support," which was not a shock, but the papers said, "for Terry Allen, Gloria Jean, Larry Michael, *and Keith Allan* Haataja." Evidently, when Nels and

Eileen pulled me out of the theatre in 1952 and Eileen said, "We're going to be a family again," she was under the impression that Nels had left his mistress. Although I have no proof, I think it's safe to say that Nels had probably returned to ask Eileen for a divorce. Before dropping the hammer, however, he had decided to have a little fun with her. That he should have had his fun at the Honkala's home, the aunt and uncle of the woman he ran off with, is ironic, to say the least. Eileen must have been totally in the dark about their role in all of this. The pregnancy, of course, explains why Eileen stopped visiting us and why she signed our release papers. She had given birth to Keith approximately thirty-five days before I saw her at the convent, which also explains the fullness of her figure.

Three months after learning of Keith's existence, I located him in Milwaukee, Wisconsin. According to Keith, he had lived with a couple by the name of Elmer and Mae (Lillian) Larson from 1953 to 1956. He doesn't know if they are related, or if they were foster parents. Whatever the relationship, the photos suggest that Eileen must have had visitation rights, as the one showing her holding Keith reads, "6½ months."

In 1956, a family from Fairmont, Minnesota, adopted Keith. We have sent each other e-mails and photos, but we still have not met. Perhaps someday we will.

What role did Alfred and Martha Honkala play in the family drama? If there are villains in this tragedy, they are perhaps the Honkalas. My research found that they had quite an infamous past. In March of 1943, while Martha was in town having an illegal abortion, a blizzard hit the Duluth area, laying down twenty-five inches of snow in three days, closing schools and institutions, downing power lines, stranding motorists, and marooning families in their homes. On the second day of the storm, the police received a call about seven children stranded in a farmhouse. The police, following snowplows, worked their way to the house. When they arrived, they found the front door ajar, snow piled high in the living room, and seven cold and hungry children huddled together for warmth. The baby's diaper was frozen and one of the boys was shoeless. Because this wasn't the first time Martha had abandoned the children, she received a three-month jail sentence and the state placed the children in foster and adoptive homes. Alfred, who was working at the time, was also incarcerated but for a crime unrelated to the abandonment issue. It wasn't the first time for him, nor would it be the last. Martha would later give birth to three more children: a boy, who survived the abortion attempt but later died of pneumonia, and two girls—the two sisters I met in 1952.

My investigation into Nels's background suggests that he and Alfred probably met in 1947 while working at the steel mill in Morgan Park. As my research widened, I learned that there was more to the relationship then drinking. It turns out the Honkalas were related to the woman that Nels ran off with and they may have actually introduced her to him. The introduction most likely took place in December of 1947 or in January of the following year. The date is significant because she gave birth to a baby girl in August of 1948, and from what little Nels told me, he consented to the use of his name on the birth certificate. This drama, of course, was unfolding while we were living with him in Morgan Park. The woman's pregnancy, I would learn, had resulted from a rape, not from the union with Nels, but I was not able to determine if he knew about the rape before he consented to the use of his name, or if that fact came out later. When I met him in 1975, he told me he had one adopted daughter and four natural children by this woman. I got the impression he had a good relationship with the adopted daughter—perhaps better than with the rest of his children. Did Alfred and Martha use Nels to help their relative out of a jam, or was Nels playing the part of a gentleman? I'll never know, and at this stage, it's not important. What's important is that what happened to my sister and me, and for this, perhaps, I should "thank" the Honkalas.

Did Lillian Larson subconsciously want me out of the way? Why Lillian put Larry and me in the unheated hallway and why she waited so long to get help is a question that bothers me to this day. There was plenty of room in Alan's bedroom for two Army cots. Why didn't she put us in there? From what I've been able to learn, there are three possible answers.

First, there's the question of who called the shots, and the obvious answer is Grandma. She made the decision to put us in the hallway, and she insisted that we go back to the orphanage and not to the hospital in Cook. Did she truly not know the dangers of placing two young children on Army cots, in an unheated room, in the dead of winter? I seriously doubt it. She had raised three children of her own in that house and she had grown up in that extreme setting. I have long believed that, at some level, she wanted us out of the way. She didn't wake up one day and say, "I'm going to kill my grandchildren," but she may have reasoned that, with us out of the picture, her daughter would be able to take care of one child. I know that my grandparents didn't trust Eileen to make good decisions. That was obvious from the way they treated her in front of us, and in many ways, she had proved them right. Did Grandma think it would be easier on her daughter to lose her children to a natural catastrophe than to have them taken away, knowing they were still alive?

This brings me to the second possible answer. Approximately fifteen years after I met Alan, he sent me Grandma Lillian's medical records. The main reason most orphans give for looking up their biological parents is to learn something about the family medical history: incidences of mental illness, cancer, diabetes, heart failure, etc. Although not my primary motive for finding Eileen and her family, it had certainly entered my mind.

As it turned out, Lillian's records are a gold mine of information. They go back several generations and include both the Larson and Beatty sides of the family. The record states that Lillian first noticed lumps in her right breast in August of 1950, but, as she wrote, she had "always had the idea I was going to have cancer of the right breast because I had trouble nursing: very painful – inverted nipples." That insight came in 1924 when she was thirty years old.

The significance of the cancer isn't completely clear, but it does offer a plausible explanation for why she couldn't care for us anymore. It also accounts for why Eileen's visits became less frequent—she had lost her support system. I did not remember Grandma taking us out of the orphanage for a day in 1952 (see Part V photo), but Alan and Grandma probably dropped by on their way back from the Mayo Clinic in Rochester, Minnesota, where she was being treated.

Grandma died in 1954 at the age of sixty. Was she distracted and physically exhausted during the Christmas season of 1950? Is this why she made the decision to have us sleep on Army cots in an unheated room? It goes a long way toward explaining why we left the farm for the second time, but intentionally putting us in an unheated room due to stress associated with cancer is, by itself, a stretch.

The third possibility is pride. Grandma tended to keep things to herself, especially problems within her immediate family. I didn't learn until 2007 that she hadn't even told her own parents or siblings about her daughter's problems until it was too late to intervene. According to at least one senior member of the Beatty clan, they didn't learn about our adoption until after Lillian's death, which implies that there was some shaming going on as well. That included her sister Margaret, who was a nurse at the hospital in Cook. Had they taken us there, Margaret would have learned about the orphanage. Did Grandma wait and then send us back to the Children's Home out of pride, or was it a financial decision?

I'll never know with absolute certainly if she intentionally put us in harm's way, but my gut has always leaned in the direction of infanticide. I think she loved her daughter. She wanted to protect her even at the cost of losing two of her grandchildren.

Was the Children's Home a blessing or a curse? The first thing people ask when I tell them that I lived in an orphanage is, "Oh, that must have been horrible. Were you abused?" The answer to both is a resounding no! I didn't particularly care for Mrs. Scheidler, and I didn't think Mr. Kolander was fair when it came to handing out discipline, but they weren't abusive. Solving problems with boxing gloves is prohibited today, but I've run into some people who believe we should return to those days, and there might be some merit to that way of thinking, especially as it concerns boys.

In many ways, the Children's Home functioned more like a day care than an orphanage. Formally opened on June 4, 1904, the home's mission was to provide a refuge for babies and young children whose parents were temporarily unable to give them proper care. The babies, however, had to be at least six months old. Its mission effectively limited problems associated with teenagers and with newborns. Unlike state-run orphanages, the home not only put a limit on age but it also limited the numbers of children who could be cared for at any given time. According to an article I found, during one twelve-month period the home cared for four hundred and sixty-five children, but the numbers did not exceed one hundred at any given time. Thus, our three-year stay was an exception.

The one regret I have concerns education. The home did not provide a structured environment for study, and the staff did not encourage or help the children with their homework. Because of this and the other problems I had during my stay, I fell behind, and it would take the gift of a very special teacher to get me back on track.

The organization that funded and ran the orphanage closed the Children's Home in 1956. It changed its mission and moved to a new facility called Northwood Children's Services, where it provides "professional care, education, and treatment for boys and girls with emotional, behavioral, and learning disabilities." Bless you and thank you for caring for my siblings and me during those difficult times.

What happened to the dream of a horse and a far off prairie? As for Jean and me, a farm couple from Wendell, Minnesota, a small town close to the North and South Dakota border, adopted us on July 14, 1953. The shoreline of Lake Agassiz, at one time the largest body of fresh water in the world, borders the eastern edge of the farm, and from the beachhead, I could see for miles across the Red River Valley. The view reminded me of that dream I had had as a young orphan boy sitting on the window ledge in the Naughty Room—the dream of standing next to a horse and looking over a distant prairie. The horse I dreamed of roamed freely in a pasture across the road from the farm. I never got a chance to stand next to him while I looked across the prairie, but everything else in the dream turned out to be real.

As I've said before, Jean and I have always considered ourselves fortunate to have gotten a new lease on life, and in the end things turned out for the best. Jean, who has always had both of her feet planted firmly on the ground, adapted quickly to our new environment. I, on the other hand, continued to react defensively to every insult that offended my sensibility, but that's a subject for another time.

Photo of the author and his sister with their adoptive parents taken in 1964 on the front steps of the Lawrence Presbyterian Church near Wendell, Minnesota.

About The Author

Terry Degner is a husband, father, and grandfather of fifteen children. He is by now an expert on family dynamics. For over twenty-three years, he designed, wrote, directed, and edited hundreds of video, sound, and multimedia productions; including children's shows, documentaries, dramas, and training and promotional programs. For twelve of those years, he owned and managed his own production company, and his skill at writing is what brought in the repeat business. In addition to his media career, the author spent twelve years in sales and marketing, climbing the corporate ladder and winning many awards along the way. He got an education in electronics from the U.S. Navy, a degree from the University of Minnesota in broadcasting journalism, and he is a certified webmaster. Terry was ideally suited to write, with captivating dialogue, this true account of his life to the age of eight—a goal he set for himself at the age of twelve.

CPSIA information can be obtained at www.ICGtesting.com
Printed in the USA
BVOW070528261011

274495BV00001B/3/P